W9-BOA-906

— PERIOD—
KITCHENS

—PERIOD—
KITCHENS

A PRACTICAL GUIDE TO
PERIOD-STYLE DECORATING

Judith Miller

MITCHELL BEAZLEY

First published in Great Britain in 1995 by Mitchell Beazley
an imprint of Reed Consumer Books Limited
Michelin House, 81 Fulham Road
London SW3 6RB
and Auckland, Melbourne, Singapore and Toronto

Chief Contributor: **John Wainwright**

Editor: **Nina Sharman**
Art Editor: **Lisa Tai**
Production: **Heather O'Connoll**

Executive Editor: **Judith More**
Art Director: **Jacqui Small**
Executive Art Editor: **Larraine Shamwana**

Special photography: **Michael Crockett**
Colour Illustrations: **Coral Mula**
Jacket photographs: **James Merrell**

A CIP record for this book is available from the British Library

ISBN 1 85732 398 X

The publishers have made every effort to ensure that all instructions given in this book
are accurate and safe, but they cannot accept liability for any resulting injury, damage or
loss to either person or property whether direct or consequential and howsoever arising.

Produced by Mandarin Offset
Printed and bound in Hong Kong

Contents

Foreword

During the latter part of the 20th century the kitchen has gradually become, in many respects, the most important room in the house. The money spent by many homeowners on furnishing and decorating this room alone can often match or even exceed the combined financial outlay on all of the other rooms put together.

There have been a number of reasons for this development. Firstly, there has been a widespread and understandable desire to modernize, especially after the Second World War, which has entailed the removal of fixtures and fittings thought to be antiquated or obsolete and to replace them with the latest developments that technology and design have to offer.

Secondly, the demands of a typical 20th-century lifestyle, in which most adults in the household go out to work, and where cooks or maids are a thing of the past, have resulted in labour-saving devices for the kitchen – washing machines, dishwashers, refrigerators, freezers, microwaves, ovens or stoves with automatic timing devices, and food mixers – becoming not so much a luxury as a practical necessity. The purchase and installation of such appliances has naturally been accompanied by an ever-increasing emphasis on the layout of the kitchen. Cupboards/cabinets, work counters, eating areas, wall and floor coverings are all designed and combined to produce ergonomically efficient and hygienic surroundings for the storage, preparation, cooking and eating of food.

Thirdly, a substantial number of appliance manufacturers and design companies have emerged to meet the demand for new kitchens. Consistent and widespread advertising of new products and services in newspaper colour supplements and weekly and monthly magazines has undoubtedly elevated a new kitchen to not only a practical necessity but also an object of desire and a status symbol.

To condemn this process of modernization on purist grounds would be to misunderstand the nature of housing in general and kitchens in particular. Historically, both have gradually evolved over time to meet the changing requirements of new homeowners. Continual updating, renewal and taking advantage of new technology was as familiar to the Elizabethans, the Georgians and the Victorians as it is to us in the 20th century. Moreover, no one would want to go back to cooking over an open hearth just because they live in a Tudor or early Georgian house.

Whether you like or dislike particular changes is a matter of personal aesthetics. However, since around the end of the 1970s there has been a fairly broad consensus that many modernized kitchens have been unsympathetic to the structure and style of the period house. Put more simply, much of the original "character" of the house has been stripped away. A typical example would be a hi-tech kitchen featuring built-in plastic laminated cupboards/cabinets with a stainless steel sink that had been installed in an 19th-century country cottage or farmhouse. Such a kitchen would be more suitable for a 20th-century modernist or post-modern urban interior.

As a consequence of the reaction to unthinking modernization, homeowners and property developers alike have set about restoring many original features and redecorating in styles more appropriate to the period of the house. There is no doubt that this has been an almost universally popular development – certainly if judged only by the fact that "authentically restored" houses often command higher prices than those that have been, in estate agent's (realtor's) parlance, "completely modernized".

As more and more homeowners come to realize that such restorations not only improve their immediate surroundings, but are also a satisfying and rewarding activity in themselves, there has been a commensurate growth in the number of companies making kitchen components tailored to different types of period homes. Creating a kitchen that is in sympathy with the original architecture and character of a property – without having to forsake the advantages of modern appliances – is thus not only desirable, but also increasingly easy to achieve. I hope that this book will make that process even easier.

JUDITH MILLER

Introduction

In some smaller houses in medieval England the kitchen and the hall were combined. However, in most dwellings – both grand and humble – the kitchen was detached from the main building. The advantages of cooking in a "house" (*domo*) separated from the residential areas of the home was that it kept cooking smells isolated, minimized the risk of any kitchen fire spreading (early kitchens were made of highly combustible plastered wood), and gave closer access to an external water supply (usually from a well).

Given the flimsy nature of their construction, none of these early wooden-built kitchens have survived. However, archaeological excavations and local records have given us an insight into their make-up. Typical examples include a 13th-century detached kitchen at Weoley Castle in Birmingham, England. Measuring approximately 12 x 6.5m/40 x 22ft, it had weather-boarded walls and a reed-thatched roof, and incorporated a great hearth; access to the castle's great stone hall was via a pentize (a covered walkway). A detached, timber-framed kitchen at Northolt Manor, in Middlesex, England, appears to have been of similar construction. Dating from c. 1300–50, and measuring some 2.8sq.m/30sq.ft, it featured a central hearth and a post hole for a spit or firehood. Its western quadrant had a roughly tiled floor; most of the cooking, however,

seems to have been done outside in a large pebbled area with a number of open hearths.

Not surprisingly, the few kitchens that have survived from the medieval era were made of stone and attached to large manor houses, monasteries, castles and palaces. For example, at Gillingham, a royal residence in Kent, the kitchen built *c.*1260 was sited a short distance away from the end wall of the great hall, with a passage leading to it between the pantry and buttery. A scullery (*herlebecheria*) may have also been added on the outside. Perhaps the most impressive surviving example is the Abbot's Kitchen at Glastonbury, England. Dating from the middle of the 14th century, it is square externally, octagonal inside, measures 10m/33ft across and reaches to the full height of the rest of the building. The fireplaces, which were used to cook on and heat water for well over three hundred people, are set in the angles of the octagonal.

THE MIDDLE AGES

During the Middle Ages the kitchen gradually began to be integrated with the rest of the house, although this process was not fully complete until the 16th century. Most kitchens tended to be either square or oblong in shape (although some of the earlier examples still had an octagonal timber roof), and in larger dwellings were sited in

Left: *This 17th-century open hearth in the kitchen of a house in New York incorporates a small "beehive" oven in the back wall, primarily used for making bread. The hinged, cast-iron crane on the right was designed to support pots and kettles over the fire, and could be swung through 90 degrees to allow the householder to fill and empty pots without having to stoop into the hearth. Many fireplaces of this size would have had a pair of cranes on either side of the hearth.*

Right: *The late Victorian kitchen of a large house in Scotland. An increased understanding of, and concern about, hygiene during the latter half of the 19th century resulted in the establishment of separate work surfaces for the preparation of meat and other ingredients. Although there is some open shelving in this kitchen, the shelves of the large freestanding dresser are enclosed, and consequently used for the storage of a fine-quality dinner service, which would not have been required for daily use, and only brought out on special occasions.*

line beyond the butteries. By the 15th century most fireplaces were no longer centrally placed open hearths, but built at the end wall of the range and had large flues and chimneys above to carry away the smoke and hot gases. Also, in larger houses it became more usual to place the kitchen in an extension of the butteries, at right angles to the hall block, thereby forming an L-shape. Access was either through a side door from the butteries, or from the back entrance of the hall. An alternative arrangement, as at Bowhill House, Exeter, England, was to site the kitchen in a range parallel to the hall, their doorways facing across the court and the two blocks joined by long ranges containing a parlour, butteries, food storage departments, a brew house and bakery, with various chambers sited on a second floor.

THE 16TH AND 17TH CENTURIES
Although its shape and position in relation to the rest of the house may have changed, the 16th-and indeed 17th-century kitchen differed little from its predecessors as a working environment. Walls were limewashed plaster, and decoration, if any, was limited to simple stencilling. In the humblest abodes, floors were either of beaten earth, plaster mixed with straw or, in rural areas where livestock were kept inside during the winter, cobblestones. In many of the more affluent dwellings bricks, laid on edge, or tiles (sometimes

glazed and patterned) were used underfoot. Stone slabs, granite and slate, usually quarried locally, were the preferred option during the Tudor and Jacobean periods (1485–1625), and in grander houses were either painted or covered in rush matting. In the British Isles and throughout most of Europe, wood was rarely used for flooring in kitchens. However, some early 17th-century kitchens in the American colonies did have close-grained, butt-jointed, bare boards.

Prior to the end of the 17th century, kitchen furniture in most houses was a mixture of built-in and free-standing, and kept to a minimum. In addition to the odd free-standing cupboard or dresser, the most common form of storage unit remained the medieval aumbry, which took the form of either a frame or door attached to a shelved recess in a wall, or a top-lifting bin (designed to protect food from rodents). In many houses built during the 16th and 17th centuries these cupboards were ventilated, some externally and many with pierced perforations in the internal wooden doors. In smaller houses and cottages, particularly in rural areas, where the kitchen also served as a communal living space, householders ate at a large trestle table (also used for the preparation of food) in the middle of the room, and sat on benches or back-stools.

Apart from the light emitted from the hearth, artificial lighting prior to the 18th century was

Left: *Castle Drogo in Devon, England, was designed in 1910 by Edwin Lutyens, and was equipped with this spacious, top-lit, granite-lined kitchen. The large work table, with its detach-able, curved wooden chopping boards, is, like the rest of the kitchen, built on a baronial scale, and was designed to allow up to three or four members of the kitchen staff to prepare the numerous dishes and serv-ings required in a house of this size. The built-in wooden dressers allow ingredients and much of the batterie de cuisine to be kept in view and close to hand; the work surfaces above the drawers and cupboards also providing additional areas for the preparation of food. Aside from the enclosed cast-iron range, the over-head electric lights and the internal telephone, Lutyens's inspiration can be found in the castle kitchens of medieval Europe.*

largely restricted to beeswax candles (held in lanterns and wall-sconces) and rush-lights in bet-ter houses, while more humble dwellings made do with a combination of rush lights and tallow dips – the latter giving off a rather unpleasant smell. In the American Colonies early settlers relied on rush lights, oil lamps, Betty lamps (boat-shaped lamps filled with oil) or candles.

Throughout this period, cooking took place on spits or in a variety of skillets and other pots and pans placed on grids over open fires and hearths. In many rural dwellings, large, woodburning inglenook fireplaces became increasingly com-mon and were incorporated into new and existing, houses. Their fires, which were usually kept permanently alight from autumn (fall) through to spring, provided much-needed warmth in households where the kitchen and hall, living-room or parlour were one and the same.

However, the cosy notion of the family or ser-vants gathered around the kitchen fire, well-fed and warmed from the cold outside, is somewhat misleading. For those who had to work in them, most pre-18th-century kitchens tended to be too warm in summer and too cold and damp in win-ter. Lighting was rarely adequate, labour-saving devices were few and far between, smoke often blew back into the room from the fire, and water and fuel had to be constantly fetched from out-side. Such conditions, were exacerbated in those kitchens that began to be sited "below stairs" – in the cellars and basements of new houses spring-ing up in the expanding cities and towns of the late 17th and early 18th centuries.

THE 18TH CENTURY

In many respects the kitchen as we know it to-day began to emerge during the 18th century.

Improvements in working conditions were minimal at first, and even by the end of the century, artificial lighting was no more advanced than it had been previously. However, the arrival of coal as a fuel for cooking led initially to the development of raised roasting hearths which, like their predecessors, still incorporated spits, but later began to evolve into the theoretically more efficient cast-iron cooking range. Shallow stone or lead sinks, sited under a single cold-water tap or faucet fed either by tank water or a very rudimentary public supply in some towns and cities, also began to appear in some Georgian houses.

As the range of kitchenwares and utensils increased throughout the 18th century, the attendant need for more storage and work space was met by a variety of tall cupboards and sturdy oak and elm dressers, the latter often incorporating drawers and surmounted by graduated shelving. Made of softwoods such as pine, these items tended to be painted for ease of cleaning, and styled to match the wooden wall panelling that gradually took over from limewashed plaster walls in many of the more affluent households in urban and rural areas. Fixed wooden work surfaces, usually supported on turned balusters, also began to appear in some urban kitchens.

Among other 18th-century improvements was a more widespread use of floor coverings to ameliorate the chill of stone, bricks and tiles underfoot. Painted floorcloths embellished with, for example, stencils or marbled diamond patterns were typical, although rush matting and rag rugs were also in common use – the latter particularly in the American Colonies. (Crumb cloths were also placed on top of floorcloths to protect them from spillage and general wear and tear.) Wooden floors, which had hitherto largely been confined to American Colonial houses, were installed in some new urban houses in Britain, and were usually made from deal (fir or pine), either stained and polished or painted and varnished.

THE FIRST HALF OF THE 19TH CENTURY

Given the tremendous advances in manufacturing, design and technology, improvements in the kitchen were relatively slow to materialize during the first half of the 19th century. In grander rural houses, and middle- and upper-middle-class urban dwellings, progress largely concentrated on the replacement of traditional open-hearth methods of cooking and heating water with the cast-iron, coal-burning kitchen range. First patented in 1780 by Thomas Robinson, the basic

Left: *A late-19th-century kitchen dresser, in a house in Glasgow, Scotland. The built-in coal-bunker would have serviced the cast-iron cooking range.*

Above: *A built-in dresser, c.1720s from the kitchen of a house in Spitalfields, London, with graduated shelves, baluster supports and open storage below.*

design for this new appliance was to remain largely unaltered for nearly a hundred years. Although theoretically more efficient, most of the early ranges were actually as labour-intensive to run as previous and more primitive methods of cooking. Moreover, they were prone to unexpected variations in temperature or suddenly going out, and could make kitchens insufferably hot during the summer months.

Poor working conditions for the cook and other household servants were undoubtedly exacerbated by the fact that family life in many early Victorian households revolved around the parlour rather than the kitchen hearth. With the exception of country cottages, farmhouses, and urban working-class and lower-middle-class homes, in which it remained the principal "living room", the kitchen and its ancillary larders, pantries, sculleries and store rooms, was sited in the basement. Later in the century, following the passage of various Health Acts and Local Authority Bye-Laws in Britain in the 1860s, which discouraged the use of basements as habitable rooms, kitchens were frequently located in extensions at the back of the house.

The advantage to the homeowner of locating the kitchen in the basement or a back extension was that, as with the detached kitchens of the Medieval period and the Middle Ages, the family

and guests, not to mention fabrics and other furnishings, could be isolated from the heat, grease and smells generated by the preparation of food. The disadvantage to the servants was that such kitchens were still often poorly lit, inadequately ventilated, damp, and too hot or too cold depending on the time of year.

In Britain, Europe and prior to the Civil War in North America, such kitchens housed only the most basic of creature comforts. In these utilitarian spaces servants carried out endless strenuous tasks, such as preparing food, scouring pots and skillets or pans, stoking and blacking the cast-iron range, heating water, scrubbing floors and washing and ironing household linen. The fact that the widespread availability of inexpensive servant labour meant that the housewife and other members of better-off families could keep out of the kitchen goes a long way to explaining why comfort and convenience were fairly slow in coming to this part of the Victorian home.

THE SECOND HALF OF THE 19TH CENTURY

If lack of progress in kitchen design and technology during the first half of the 19th century was largely due to the kitchen being out of sight and therefore out of mind for the homeowner, notable improvements made from the 1860s onward were stimulated by more than just the return (to

Above: *A late 19th-century, cast-iron range, by Abendroth Brothers of New York. The decorative mouldings are typical of the Beaux Arts era, although not as ornate as some of the neo-Classical detailing and latticework found on other ranges of the period.*

Above: *The "Eagle" combination grate of c.1935 incorporated within a single unit a fireplace with a back boiler and a number of ovens for cooking. The tiled surround and hearth were typical of combination grates – a 20th-century version of the old Dutch oven.*

a limited extent) of the lady of the house down-stairs. Changes in social attitudes toward the role of women and servants, increased understanding of the importance of hygiene, technological innovations and fashionable ideas about kitchen decoration and design also played their part.

For most of the first half of the 19th century, the lady of the house (in grander homes) had confined herself to planning menus for the week with the cook, overseeing the purchase of provisions and, in some cases, keeping books and instructing new servants on the particular requirements of the household. However, servants gradually became harder to find. In the United States this was partly a result of the abolition of slavery at the end of the Civil War, while on both sides of the Atlantic there was also the effect of the financial attraction of jobs in the ever-increasing number of new factories. Combined with the growth of the new middle classes, who could afford fewer servants than the rich, the result was that more and more women across society found themselves having to spend more and more time in the kitchen. Although in many cases their activities were confined to making bread and training staff, as they increasingly began to work alongside their servants, improvements in comfort, convenience and cleanliness soon followed. Such changes also resulted from a growing concern about the welfare of servants and the conditions under which they worked. This was evident in the recommendations of influential writers in Britain, such as Mrs Beeton, who emphasized the importance of cleanliness in the kitchen: a dirty fire meant a dirty kitchen, as did the presence of mice, rats and cockroaches. Popular women's magazines in the United States also promulgated newly fashionable notions such as "the house is not furnished whose kitchen has not received the same attention as a kitchen that its parlour receives as a parlour".

The introduction of mains water under pressure, gas and plumbed-in sinks and boilers to many urban and rural houses during the 1860s and 1870s, together with the increasing availability of a variety of proprietary cleaning products, also contributed to the later Victorian kitchen becoming a more hygienic and pleasant place to work in than it had been previously.

However, the heart of the late Victorian kitchen, as it had been during the first half of the 19th century, was the cast-iron range. Early models consisted of a coal fire contained by the horizontal bars of a grate. Kettles and pots and pans rested on a hinged tip-bar and hung from a variety of hooks, cranes and trivets over the fire – the latter often being open to the chimney. On one side of the fire was a range for baking, which

Left: *The "Imperial Gas Cooking Stove" from Nicholl and Clarke's catalogue of 1906. The last word in technology for its time, it incorporated a tank of water in the hood, which was heated by the oven. The water was then circulated to a tap or faucet on the side of the oven, and to the hot water tap over the kitchen sink.*

Above right: *An early electric stove, c.1913, from the American "General Electric" range.*

Right: *A gas range, with a grill/broiler at the base, manufactured by George M. Clark of Chicago, c.1889.*

Above: *A small, freestanding electric cooker from the 1930s. Sparsely ornamented, it has a four-ring hob/cooktop and a single, thermostatically controlled oven and grill/broiler.*

Left: *Made during the first quarter of the 19th century, these built-in cupboards/ cabinets embody many of the principles of design and craftsmanship promulgated by the Arts and Crafts Movement. Constructed of fine-quality seasoned wood, and showing a high level of craftsmanship, they are well-proportioned, practical and aesthetically pleasing.*

Left: *One wall of a 1950s built-in kitchen. The large, inset china sink has been sited under the window in order to maximize the level of natural light when wash- ing up. The tiled work surface and splashback introduce colour and pat- tern that provides an attractive contrast to the cream-painted cupboards/ cabinets, drawers and walls. Although durable and hygienic, the tiled work sur- face is not ideal for all aspects of food preparation, and has thus sensibly been augmented with wooden chopping boards.*

in later 19th-century models was surrounded by a flue through which hot gases passed before entering the chimney, thereby providing a more even distribution of heat. The cook could also adjust the temperatures in the stove by opening and closing a selection of dampers and bypass flues. A tank for heating water was positioned on the other side of the fire, the water obtained via a tap or faucet in some models and a ladle in others. (Toward the end of the 19th century, following the widespread installation of mains water under pressure, many such tanks incorpo- rated a ballcock to allow automatic, rather than manual filling with cold water.)

On early ranges, joints of meat were roasted on a spit over the fire, with trays placed under- neath to catch the melting fat and juices. The more expensive models featured cheeks at the

Above: *A kitchen "planned on American lines" in a house at Gribloch, Stirlingshire, designed by Basil Spence in 1938. A white-enamelled, cast-iron Aga – the 20th-century* *successor to the Victorian range – sits comfortably in this streamlined Modernist layout where rows of cupboards/cabinets support long work surfaces and two stainless steel sinks.*

sides of the grate which could be adjusted to increase the width of radiant heat and so accommodate large joints; vanes within the chimney were turned by the draft in the flue and caused a horizontal spit to rotate via a series of connecting gears and pulleys. On less sophisticated early ranges, a vertical spit was turned by a bottle jack – a clockwork motor set in a bottle-shaped brass case – usually suspended from the mantel shelf above, and semi-circular metal reflectors, known as "hasteners", were used to concentrate the heat from the fire on the slowly turning joint.

However, more advanced models, such as "the kitchener", produced later in the 19th century, enclosed the fire beneath a hot plate. This arrangement, which required less coal to produce the same amount of heat, forced all the hot gases from the fire up through a system of flues to heat the range and the boiler, instead of letting them go straight up the chimney as with earlier models.

As in previous centuries, the main work surface in the late-Victorian kitchen consisted of a large central table. Usually made of deal, and scrubbed down daily, it incorporated shallow drawers for kitchen utensils and was surrounded by an assortment of chairs on which servants sat to eat their meals. Other tables included a small, marble-topped one for rolling out pastry and a long wooden one positioned next to the sink (provided the latter was not installed in the scullery, as was usually the case in larger houses) for

draining dishes. "Built-in" work-tops or counters were still quite rare, although toward the end of the century they did increasingly feature, along with a range of high-quality built-in cupboards/cabinets and shelving, in Arts and Crafts style kitchens installed in some of the more affluent urban households.

In most late Victorian houses, storage tended to be a combination of freestanding cupboards, cabinets, dressers and open shelving. The main advantage of the latter was that it promoted efficiency, as virtually everything necessary for the orderly running of the kitchen was visible and easily to hand. However, the disadvantage to open display, was that it exposed kitchen utensils and storage tins and jars to moisture, grease and dust. The solution to this dilemma was the glass-fronted cabinet, which became increasingly popular, especially in urban households, toward the end of the century.

Other storage furniture found in Victorian households included a meat or pie safe – a freestanding cabinet with wire windows, used to protect cooked meats and pies from flies – and an icebox. The latter, which in the 1840s had been little more than a simple wooden box in which food was placed on a block of ice, had evolved by the 1860s into an insulated wooden cabinet filled with crushed ice – a prototype refrigerator.

As in previous centuries, the number of ancillary rooms leading from the kitchen depended on the size of house. Almost all homes had a scullery, which contained a sink, a wooden draining board and a large wooden plate rack on the wall above. In houses where there was not room for a separate laundry, the scullery also contained a large wash copper, set into brickwork over a fire. Some sculleries even housed a second stove or range, which was used for heating water and flat irons. In addition to washing up, laundering and ironing, the scullery was also used for cleaning silver, polishing brass and peeling vegetables, as well as providing storage for larger pots and pans and household cleaning equipment.

As well as a storeroom or larder (of which there was more than one in larger houses) set off the scullery, many homes also had a butler's pantry. Located in-between the kitchen and the dining room, the pantry was usually connected to the latter via a dumb waiter, provided storage space for tableware, dishes and glasses in ceiling-high cupboards (usually glass-fronted), and allowed a space for making the finishing touches to dishes before they were sent upstairs. The pantry also housed a "call box" – a system for summoning servants to other parts of house: when a cord was pulled or a bell pushed, a number popped up in a box informing staff which room required service.

Floors in the Victorian kitchen were much the same as in previous centuries: stone, brick, tiles, wood or, in the grandest houses, marble. Tile inserts were often sited beneath the range to guard against fire. Floorcloths, rag rugs and crumb cloths were also popular. Linoleum became increasingly popular toward the end of the century, and was recommended by Mrs Beeton as both hard-wearing and hygienic.

There were also improvements in lighting from the 1860s onward, the widespread intro-

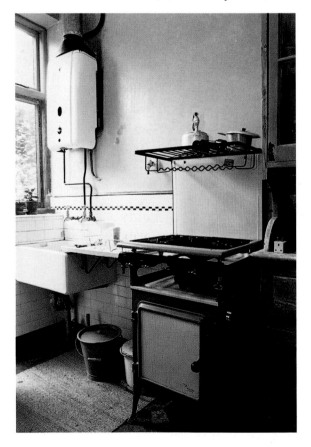

Above: *A corner of a 1930s English kitchen. The antithesis of the Modernist kitchen shown on page 9, it features a china sink supported on wall brackets, and* a freestanding gas cooker and painted dresser. The complete absence of co-ordinating decoration and style is offset by the convenience of juxtaposition.

duction of gas lamps into upper- and middle-class homes helping to improve the gloom, particularly where the kitchen and its ancillary rooms were sited below stairs. However, it was only with the advent of electricity in the 1880s that artificial illumination reached a level commensurate with that found in 20th-century kitchens.

THE 20TH CENTURY

Major developments in the kitchen during the 20th century have been influenced by two main factors: further, and considerable, advances in technology, coupled with a concerted and successful attempt by architects and designers to produce an ergonomically efficient and pleasant working environment that meets the needs of modern family life.

As far as technology is concerned, a reliable supply of electricity and/or gas to most homes, however remote their location, has resulted in the production of increasingly sophisticated electric and gas stoves, ranging from the Aga (also available in coal, wood and oil-burning form, and a direct descendant of the cast-iron range) to the separate hob/cooktop and self-cleaning, fan-assisted oven. In addition, electric-powered extractor units have improved air quality, and a wide range of devices – including, among many, the refrigerator, freezer, dishwasher, washing machine, food-mixer, waste-disposal/garbage-disposal unit, electric kettle and toaster – have proved to be labour-saving and invaluable to today's busy modern families.

Similarly, the development of new materials, such as stainless steel, plastics and vinyl, has led to the development of durable, easy-to-clean (and therefore more hygienic) floor coverings and work surfaces. The use of laminated composite materials such as chipboard and MDF (medium density fibreboard), rather than solid wood, has made it both easier and less costly to produce matching, modular cupboards and cabinets for storing kitchen utensils and food and housing built-in appliances. The 20th-century kitchen is also more than adequately lit following the development of the electric light – ranging from Edison's carbon-filament lamp at the beginning of the century, to fluorescent tubes in the 1940s, spotlights in the 1950s and low-voltage halogen lights in the 1970s, the latter rendering large lighting fixtures unnecessary and making it possible to install spotlights and lighting tracks virtually out of sight. Moreover, the mass-production of all of these new materials and appliances has helped to keep their costs down to levels affordable to most householders.

The ever-increasing mechanization of the kitchen has, since the 1920s and 1930s, been accompanied by various notable changes in lay-out and design. At the heart of this lies the Modern Movement's revival of the neo-Classical ideal of a completely co-ordinated room. In most households since the 1920s and 1930s, the result has been an inexorable move toward the "fitted" kitchen: cupboards/cabinets, worktops or counters and appliances have increasingly been "built-in", rather than freestanding. Together they form a co-ordinated and ergonomically efficient whole in which everything needed for a particular task, whether it be making bread or chopping vegetables, is stored close to hand while leaving surrounding surfaces free from clutter.

The substantial improvements in the working environment of the 20th-century kitchen that have been made possible by new technology have also fuelled the fashion for integrating the dining area within the kitchen. While this has been the traditional arrangement in farmhouses and country cottages, in most urban and larger country dwellings it has proved to be a very useful and popular development, particularly where space is at a premium. Detaching or isolating the kitchen from the rest of the house is no longer necessary or advantageous, as it was in previous centuries – cooking smells, humidity and fluctuations in temperature having been minimized to levels unimaginable to the Medieval, or even the Victorian, householder.

Kitchenalia

One of the most effective ways of creating a period look in a kitchen is to employ period kitchenalia. In good condition, most will function as efficiently as modern equivalents. The best sources are antique shops, market stalls, auction houses, junk shops and boot fairs – but be warned: they have become quite collectable, and prices are rising.

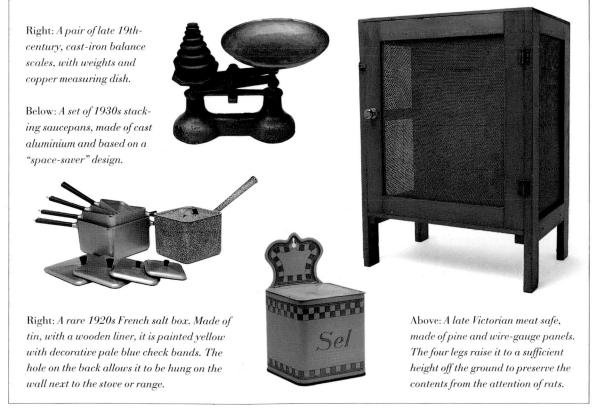

Right: *A pair of late 19th-century, cast-iron balance scales, with weights and copper measuring dish.*

Below: *A set of 1930s stacking saucepans, made of cast aluminium and based on a "space-saver" design.*

Right: *A rare 1920s French salt box. Made of tin, with a wooden liner, it is painted yellow with decorative pale blue check bands. The hole on the back allows it to be hung on the wall next to the stove or range.*

Above: *A late Victorian meat safe, made of pine and wire-gauge panels. The four legs raise it to a sufficient height off the ground to preserve the contents from the attention of rats.*

KITCHEN STYLES

Country Cottage Style

The romanticization of "cottage style" began during the second half of the 19th century. To William Morris and other members of the Arts and Crafts Movement the country cottage represented a wholesome and idyllic alternative to the increasing uniformity associated with houses in the industrialized towns and cities.

In many respects such a view was a considerable departure from reality: most of the cottages built between the 16th and 19th centuries were cramped, poorly constructed and, being designed to house the rural poor, offered only the most basic of amenities. However, the romanticized appeal of the cottage has stuck, and the 19th-century architect Charles Voysey's suggestion that people "try the effect of a well-proportioned room with white-washed walls...and simple furniture and nothing in it but necessary articles of use..." remains as an attractive proposition today as it did then. The advent of modern labour-saving devices, such as refrigerators, freezers and cookers, which can be effectively "disguised" by incorporating them into period-style cupboards/cabinets, has only added to their appeal.

The hallmark of the cottage kitchen is comfortable clutter. Set against a background of white-washed or limewashed walls, numerous items of kitchenalia are stored side-by-side with the fruits of the field and garden. Most are on open display, standing on or hanging from open shelving, exposed beams and rustic pieces of furniture. Everything combines to create a cosy and charming whole, the disparate elements are far removed from the integrated, built-in look of modern urban kitchens. The essential elements that go to make up cottage style are natural materials and simple, comfortable furniture.

Floors are of stone, brick, wood or tile. Walls are whitewashed or limewashed in earth colours, such as green or terracotta, and often decorated with folk-art stencils depicting rustic motifs such as plants, flowers and animals. These patterns and motifs are often repeated in the tiles around the sink, the tablecloth and the curtains, and sometimes run over onto individual pieces of furniture. Furniture is invariably of simple but solid construction and can be colour-washed or crudely wood-grained.

Above: *An eclectic combination of pots, pans, a cast-iron range; a wall-hung cupboard and a marble-topped desk, in different styles and from different eras – typical of the country kitchen.*

Right: *The numerous pieces of country pottery are as much a part of the decorations as the paint on the walls.*

Top: *The tiny, low-ceilinged kitchen of a potter's cottage in Surrey. At its heart is a small Aga which, in addition to the three ovens and four hotplates for cooking, also provides hot water as well as heating during the winter.*

Above left: *At the other end of the cottage kitchen shown top, drying herbs hang from an exposed cross-beam.*

Above: *A refectory table and a pair of bench seats are typical of plain and functional country furniture.*

Above: *A repeat stencil border echoes the floral-patterned, tiled splashback.*

Left: *White cupboards and a slate work surface and floor establish a cool, dairy-like feel in this Cornish kitchen.*

Below: *A 1920s Hollywood "cottage" kitchen, with a red brick floor and traditional whitewashed rafters.*

Above: *A simple Spanish country kitchen. While the cooking facilities could hardly be described as extensive, the two-ring, gas-fired cooktop is extremely versatile in the hands of a creative cook – as witnessed by the substantial array of pots and pans hung conveniently above. Where lack of space is a problem, a drop-leaf table, as here, often provides the answer.*

Right: *The seemingly disparate elements of this washing-up corner of an English farmhouse kitchen, actually combine to make a very ergonomically efficient whole. Cleaning materials and scraps go under the large china sink. Washed crockery drains in the plate rack, and is stored on the open shelves on the wall and in the cupboard to the left of the sink.*

Country House Style

Traditionally, the owners of farmhouses and manor houses have always been more affluent than cottage dwellers. Consequently, country-house kitchens, are commensurately larger than cottage kitchens, and are usually accompanied by one, two or more ancillary rooms, such as a pantry and scullery. The greater amount of space available has meant that there has been more room for cupboards/cabinets and other items of furniture, and these have, in turn, generally been more substantial and of better quality than their cottage counterparts.

However, because the kitchen is the working heart of a country house, it has still been the most practical option to store many items in daily use, such as herbs, plates, pots and pans, and a variety of utensils, close-to-hand. There is a far greater preponderance of items on open shelves and hanging from exposed beams or racks suspended from the ceiling than there is in a typical urban kitchen – although the extra space means that the average country-house kitchen is never as cluttered as a cottage kitchen.

In country-house kitchens decoration is often more formal than in country cottages. As an alternative to whitewash, walls can often be wood-panelled and painted, or even papered, and dining areas may well be carpeted.

Above: *A smart country kitchen – antiqued pine cupboards/cabinets and shelves sit happily with modern appliances and a 19th-century Windsor armchair. Dried flowers and decoy ducks add rustic charm.*

Left: *Exposed beams, a bare brick wall, niche shelving, a plate rack on the draining board, and a ladder rack for hanging kitchen utensils over a centrally placed table, are all typical elements of a traditional farmhouse kitchen.*

Above: *The combination of cream-painted walls, an inset white-enamelled sink, tongue-and grooved cabinet doors, and the blue and white English Cornishware on the window sill help to create a country dairy feel in this rural kitchen.*

Above: *A multi-functional, central island dominates the large kitchen of an English manor house. One half of it consists of a large butcher's block with cabinets under-* *neath. The other half has a granite work surface that incorporates a gas hob/cook-top. Close to hand, kitchen utensils hang from a sus-pended wooden rack.*

Above: *The washing up wall in the butler's pantry of a manor house. A large, inset china sink is flanked by wood-framed, tiled draining boards. Together with the cupboards/cabinets below and the extensive plate rack on the wall above, they are designed to cope with the washing, drying and storage of the substantial amount of crockery required in a house of this size.*

Left: *The exposed brickwork and the rough-cut wooden lintel over the old fireplace recess, which now houses an Aga, are typical rustic ele-ments that instantly locate this kitchen in the country rather than the town.*

Left: *The "kitchen corner" of a large, open plan, eat-in kitchen/living room. The built-in wooden cabinets with panelled doors, the exposed beams, the copper vessels and other openly stored kitchenware, the dried flowers and the pretty cotton-print curtains at the windows are all typical ingredients of the country kitchen. The sisal matting and the carpet runner on the floor reveal the multi-purpose nature of the room as a whole, and show that as much consideration has been given to the comforts expected of a sitting and dining room as to the practical requirements of a kitchen.*

Above and right: *Two views of the same kitchen. The large island in the middle has cupboards/cabinets under the work surface on one side, and an open space on the other. This allows the householder to prepare food either standing up or sitting down, and to use the island as a "breakfast bar". The wood and wrought iron rack suspended overhead is rather under-used, and would normally be groaning under the weight of a large* batterie de cuisine, *as well as wire baskets and dried herbs.*

Above: *An unusual Scottish manor house kitchen installed by Smallbone in "Baronial" style. An enormous enamelled cast-iron range has been inserted into the fireplace recess originally intended for open-hearth cooking. The inclusion of a large tartan-covered dining table, formal dining chairs, together with a plush carpet underfoot, a candlelit chandelier above, and hunting trophies and pictures on the walls, turn the kitchen into almost a subsidiary element of the dining area – particularly when viewed against the galleried walkway above.*

Left: *The exposed ceiling beams and the central supporting pillar reveal this as a modern country kitchen that has been installed in a converted barn.*

Country Furniture

One of the essential elements in country style is, as mentioned, simple but solid furniture. Aside from open shelving in the kitchen itself, or in ancillary rooms such as pantries, sculleries and larders, most country kitchens incorporate various pieces of freestanding furniture for storage and display, or the preparation of food.

Probably the most appropriate item is the dresser, which can vary in size, and consists of rows of shelving, sometimes graduated, mounted on top of two or more base cupboards. Dressers need not be antique and can be used to store anything from table linen to glasses or larger items such as pots and pans. Often objects on display are useful as well as being attractive. The shelves are often used to store and display collections of "best" china and crockery. Depending on the space available, dressers can be augmented with a variety of cupboards, such as tallboys or armoires. The former can include perforations or slits in the doors if perishable commodities are to be stored inside, while the latter can be lined with suitably printed or hand-painted fabric or paper and, like the dresser, are also used to store and display decorative china and glass.

Among other pieces of traditional furniture are butcher's block tables for food preparation (preferably on wheels so that they can be moved to a different position as and when desired); baker's tables, and meat safes for keeping meat and other types of food cool and free from the unwanted attention of flies and insects.

Above: *A freestanding butcher's block table. Usually made of beech or a similar close-grained hardwood, they were originally designed for cutting and chopping meat, but nowadays are also used to prepare herbs and vegetables.*

Right: *A large "Victorian-style" country kitchen. The central worktable was made by local craftsmen to the specifications of the owners of the house. The built-in cupboards were dragged by a specialist decorating company to simulate the appearance of an antique painted armoire. The use of a suspended overhead hanging rail – an increasingly common feature of domestic kitchens today – has its origins in the professional kitchens of restaurants and hotels.*

Above: *The pine buffet beneath the mirror is in fact a modern reproduction of a 19th-century baker's table.*

The glass-fronted pine dresser behind is also a modern reproduction of a late 19th-century piece.

Above: *A rather unusual, but very cleverly designed wine rack, with storage drawers and a work counter above. The sides, base and back of the rack are made from rough stone slabs – their natural chilliness helping to keep the wine cool in a part of the house that can sometimes become overly warm when meals are being cooked.*

Left: *The presence of traditional pine furniture, hand-painted, 18th-century faïence tiles, a display of decorative locally made pottery, and a terracotta-coloured brick-tile floor make sure that the modern-style cooking appliances do not detract from the period feel of this Spanish kitchen.*

Left: *A classic, freestanding pine dresser of a type to be found in many late 18th- and 19th-century country kitchens. As a means of both storing and displaying chinaware it could hardly be bettered. The rush-seated, ladder-back chairs are from the same period, and are usually made of pine or beech, and decorated with traditional buttermilk or egg tempera paint. Additional embellishments are either gilded or gold or bronze metallic-painted.*

Below: *A dresser made from a mixture of pine and other woods "salvaged" from redundant pieces of furniture and joinery elsewhere in the house. There has been a long tradition of "backstairs" joinery in rural areas, where the recycling of materials was commonplace. Note that a freezer has been cleverly concealed behind one of the middle cupboard doors.*

Left: *A plain but functional pine dresser in the kitchen of a converted Edwardian lodge in Somerset. Tongue-and-groove panelled doors are a fairly common feature of country dressers. The plain china handles on the drawers, and the hand-painted ones on the cupboards, are probably not original, but entirely in keeping with the style of the piece.*

Below right: *Made by Smallbone, this elegant freestanding dresser, based on an 18th-century design, boasts a wealth of cupboards, drawers and shelves. The attention to detail, the quality of the wood and general construction, and the well-proportioned composition of the piece as a whole, make this a dresser for the grandest of country kitchens – and one in which lack of space is not a problem.*

Left: *An early 19th-century French provincial armoire, made of pine, lined with sprigged French cotton, and used to store and display a* *fine collection of green and white glazed Provençal pottery. Pieces such as this are much in demand and fetch fairly high prices at auction.*

Traditionally, country kitchens contain pieces of furniture that have been made by local craftsmen to age-old, purposeful designs, and often they have been handed down from generation to generation. Consequently, it is quite usual to find an eclectic mix of styles from different periods: 17th-century oak settles thus stand adjacent to 18th-century elm cupboards and oak Windsor chairs, and 19th-century fruitwood dressers and pine tables. The heights are frequently uneven and painted wood is mixed with scrubbed pine. What all these pieces have in common, and part of the reason that they sit happily next to each other, is their solid, practical construction and durability.

Although country-style furniture is traditionally utilitarian, this is not to say that it is without ornamentation. On the contrary, many pieces of furniture have decorative detailing that may not be as ornate or fancy as that found on equivalent pieces in the smarter and more sophisticated interiors of town houses, but nevertheless displays a delightful rustic charm.

While many country pieces, crafted from woods, such as pine, oak, elm and a variety of fruitwoods, are simply stained in natural colours and oiled or polished to bring out the natural graining and figuring of the wood, others are colourwashed (see Period Finishes: Colourwashing, page 106) or painted using "primitive" paints made from locally available materials such as buttermilk and eggs mixed with earth-coloured pigments. These "early" paints dry to produce a smooth, flat or mid-sheen finish that have a clarity of colour rarely found in modern synthetic paints, and they mellow pleasantly with age. Country furniture was sometimes painted to cover the deficiencies of the wood but also for the sheer joy of decoration. Additional decoration on country furniture is often in the form of stencilling (see Period Finishes: Stencilling, page 110).

Above: *In front of the 18th-century pine and walnut* *dresser stands a curved, 18th-century fruitwood* *tavern table and a late 18th-century pine and* *sycamore settle cushioned with Scandinavian textiles.*

Above: *One of the main advantages offered by traditional dressers compared to many modern storage units is that most of them, while appearing bulky, are actually tall, wide and shallow, and thus do not project that far into the room.*

Right: *A Pennsylvania "Dutch" dresser and chairs in the American Museum in Bath, England. The painted earth colours provide an attractive alternative to the untreated wood look associated with the English country kitchen.*

Above: *A pine display rack, with a collection of late 19th- and early 20th-century ceramics.*

Right: *The base of a 19th-century dresser, with a small display rack and a collection of Victorian pottery.*

Above: *An English mahogany settle that has been stripped and painted with a white wood stain: the unintended result is an attractive, ghostly blue tone that is akin to the traditional limed finish usually found on oak.*

Right: *An early 20th-century, wrought-iron table with a slab marble top.*

Below: *A pair of 19th-century, Windsor-back oak armchairs – probably the most common form of seating in an English cottage and farmhouse kitchen.*

Right: *A large, freestanding storage cupboard, made of beech. The absence of venti-lation bars or holes indicates that it has not been designed* *for storing perishable food-stuffs. In larger houses, cupboards such as this were often used to store table linen and crockery.*

Left and above: *Two French country kitchens, both with rush-seated chairs and the one on the right with a typical Provençal wire rack.*

Below: *White and green painted panelling provides the backdrop to a tartan theme that takes in curtains, carpet, tiles and ceramics.*

DINING FURNITURE

In the modern household, the kitchen is often the centre of the home, the room where the family gather to eat and to talk. Kitchens have become living rooms where dinner parties can be held.

The type of table used for eating at and preparing food in a country kitchen is partly determined by the space available. Round tables on pedestal bases maximize the number of people that can be seated around them, while taking up a relatively minimal amount of floor space. Similarly, a gate-leg table allows one or two flaps to be raised during meals, and lowered at other times to increase the amount of floor space. However, the standard type of table, found in most country kitchens, is rectangular and either supported by four legs at the corners, or on two trestles at each end. If the table top is also to be used for preparing food, it should be of a durable wood, such as pine or oak, that can stand up to a daily scrubbing-down.

Traditionally, dining chairs in the kitchen are often a mix of different styles acquired over time, rather than matching sets. Windsor stick-back and wheel-back chairs are very common, as are ladder-back, rush-seated types. Benches and stools are still used, as they have been since Medieval times. Pews or high-backed settles can also be used; they have a practical advantage in that both will seat a surprising number of people.

Above: *A Victorian fruitwood kitchen table, with cutlery drawers at either end and displaying a fine patina, accompanied by a set of well-worn, painted chairs with rush seats and backs.*

Above right: *Various pieces of late 18th-century "Shendoah Valley" furniture, including a drop-leaf dining table, ladder-back chairs and a foot-stool.*

Right: *A spacious, light and airy kitchen-breakfast room. Although the cream-enamelled, cast-iron Aga, the brown tiled floor and the pine cupboard doors are all 20th century, the overall layout and style of decoration gives the room a distinctive 18th-century look.*

Above: *Below a 17th-century French iron chandelier stands a 19th-century sycamore dining table; in turn surrounded by two*

18th-century Windsor chairs and four folding chairs with wicker seats and backs. The painted grandfather clock is also 18th century.

Above: *A plank-topped kitchen table with a pair of "Country Chippendale" chairs and a pew salvaged from a Baptist church.*

Below: *A wooden settle and a selection of Windsor and wheel-back chairs provide the seating for the kitchen table. All are 19th century.*

Country-Style Storage

In addition to the various items of furniture referred to on pages 28–35, the majority of storage in country kitchens has traditionally consisted of a combination of open wooden shelving and built-in cupboards/cabinets. Open shelves are a mixed blessing: on the one hand they provide almost instant access to ingredients and cooking utensils; on the other hand they create additional work as storage jars and the like have to be cleaned more often than if they were stored away in a cupboard/cabinet. This is a problem that does not apply to open plate racks sited above sinks or drainers – a rapid turnover ensures that dust and dirt does not have much time to settle.

A variation on open shelving, and one often found in Shaker-style kitchens, is the peg rack. This can be utilized to hang individual items with handles, or small hanging shelves or cupboards. Where ceiling beams are exposed, they can be used to hang various elements from the *batterie de cuisine* over cookers, tables and other work areas.

While separate larders and pantries are mostly confined to larger houses, even the smallest of kitchens usually contains an example of what was known as an aumbry – a cupboard built into a recess in the wall. The doors can either be plain or decorated with perforated patterns which also provide ventilation for perishable contents.

Left: *In many period rural houses the kitchen was augmented with one or more adjacent ancillary rooms. Depending on the size of the houses, these could include a scullery, a pantry, a butler's pantry and even a buttery and a dairy. All were used for storage and a variety of tasks that ranged from washing up to preparing food. The pantry shown here is a typical example of such a room, in that it is equipped with open shelving for storing a variety of foodstuffs and kitchen wares. Note that, as is often the case, a sink has also been installed (on the right) – its small size suggesting its primary use is for the preparation of vegetables and herbs.*

Above: *A prettily decorated farmhouse scullery, primarily used for storing china and pottery.*

Left: *A large hanging cupboard located in the kitchen itself, rather than an ancillary room, and used to store fruit and vegetable preserves, honeys and jams and various pieces of china.*

Above: *Creamware jugs, earthenware storage jars, wicker baskets and a wall-hung wooden spice rack – typical storage vessels for a country kitchens.*

Left: *In this large, walk-in larder in a converted millhouse, the stone walls, tiled floor, and the open shelving made of Bath stone are all designed to create a cool atmosphere conducive to the preservation of stored foodstuffs.*

Country-Style Work Surfaces

In all but the very smallest of rural dwellings, the kitchen table not only serves as a place for members of the household to sit down and eat, but also traditionally doubles up as one of the most important and useful work surfaces for the preparation of meals. The size of table can vary from a small, rectangular or circular one to a long refectory table that can seat ten, twelve or more. It should preferably be made of a durable wood, such as pine, oak, maple or beech, and either sealed with a polyurethane varnish, or oiled on a reasonably regular basis, so that it can be easily cleaned and to stop it drying out and cracking.

As far as other work surfaces in a country kitchen are concerned, there is a wide range of materials available. As with kitchen tables, wood has been the traditional choice in many countries. For example, close-grained hardwoods, such as teak and maple, make the most practical choice for the grooved and slightly canted draining boards on either side of a china or enamelled cast-iron sink. Teak is particularly hard-wearing and practical for use as a work surface as it is virtually impervious to splitting and cracking, even when constantly exposed to water.

Alternatives to wood include slate, granite, marble and tiles. They are easy to clean, virtually unmatched for toughness, and all but the latter are ideal for rolling out pastry because of their smooth surface and natural coolness. However, unlike wood, if used extensively they tend to amplify sound and can create something of a cold atmosphere in what is traditionally the warm and cosy environment of a rural kitchen – although this effect is mitigated somewhat where rustic-looking, warm-coloured tiles (such as terracotta) are used. All of these surfaces are also less forgiving if glass or crockery is dropped onto them. Consequently, it is preferable to limit their use to specific task areas (or utilize them in the form of chopping boards that can be moved around as and when necessary).

Above: *Cream-coloured tiles and a built-in wooden chopping board make up the worktop/counter of a small galley kitchen – the stencilled frieze behind picks up the colour of the tiles.*

Right: *A work counter made of Cornish slate provides a durable and hygienic surface for preparing food – its natural chilliness is particularly useful for making pastry.*

Left: *Ceramic tiles are available in a wide range of traditional colours, patterns and shapes. Terracotta coloured, hexagonal tiles can be purchased glazed or unglazed. If you choose the latter for a worktop/counter they will need to be treated with a varnish or be regularly polished if they are to remain impervious to water and staining.*

Below: *A beech worktop or counter, with inset sink and supplementary chopping boards.*

Left: *The practice of recycling materials from elsewhere in the house to the kitchen has a long history in country areas. Here, the marble top, with carved decoration, from an old wash-stand has been cut down to size and re-utilized as a work counter adjacent to the sink.*

Left: *One of the advantages of using tiles, as opposed to materials such as wood, or even modern melamine, is that hot pots and pans can be placed on them direct from the hob/cooktop or oven, without causing scorching or any other form of surface damage. The disadvantage of tiles, however, is that they are very unforgiving if anything fragile, such as china or glass, is dropped on them.*

Country-Style Sinks and Taps

Sinks made of glazed stoneware or porcelain-enamelled fireclay provide the most authentic and practical choice for period-style country kitchens. Modern reproduction sinks, including "double-pot" models ideal for rinsing and draining, are available from specialist kitchen suppliers, although originals are still obtainable from salvage merchants. Provided that the glaze has not cracked or worn thin, they are as hygienic as stainless steel models. Being wider and deeper than most modern sinks, they make it easier to wash large items that will not fit in a dishwasher.

The sink should be supported on brick piers or cast-iron brackets, with a slightly overlapping, canted hardwood draining board (often made of teak or oiled maple, and secured on brackets). Alternatively, it can be mounted on top of a cupboard with its rim set below the level of the slightly overlapping worktop/drainer.

Up until the 1920s and 1930s, cross-shaped, spoke- or capstan-topped, pillar taps/faucets were almost universal, and mounted either singly (cold) or in pairs (hot and cold) on the wall. However, the influence of the Modern Movement resulted in a variety of other styles emerging: notably hot and cold mixer taps/faucets and lever-operated models, many with porcelain-enamelled spokes or levers. Mounted on the wall or the worktop/counter, they were inspired by industrial designs (for use in laboratories and hospitals) and can be turned on and off with an elbow when hands are full. A wide range of both original and reproduction examples are available. Solid brass or a brass finish is the most appropriate choice for a country kitchen, although spoke or lever-operated models should be chosen according to needs or preference rather than in accordance with strict period authenticity.

Above: *This large china pot sink is supported on whitewashed plaster piers. An advantage of this traditional method of installing a sink is that it leaves a large and easily accessible storage space between the piers.*

Left: *A large, shallow granite sink and brass lever taps/faucets are a striking feature in a modern recreation of a late 18th-century country kitchen. Both the sink and taps/faucets are reproduction.*

Above: *An inset "double-pot" china sink. Provided there is sufficient space, a double sink is more useful than a single one, as it allows a number of activities to take place at the same time. For example, vegetables can be washed in one half, while clothes soak in the other. Similarly, the double-pot is more efficient when it comes to washing and rinsing pots and pans and crockery.*

Right: *A traditional, cream-coloured, glazed earthenware pot sink, supported on bare brick piers. The shallowness of the sink can be an advantage: too deep and the result is often backache.*

Above: *Separate brass taps/ faucets provide the hot and cold water for this pot sink.*

They suit this style of sink. Mixer taps/faucets are a 20th-century invention.

Above: *A combined marble sink and grooved and canted marble drainer. In many*

Mediterranean countries, a marble work surface is often cheaper than a wooden one.

Country-Style Tiles

Since the beginning of the 20th century ceramic tiles have been widely used as splashbacks behind, above and around sinks, work surfaces and stoves or ranges. This is because they not only provide a durable, easy-to-clean, hygienic surface that is impervious to moisture and other liquids, but also because of their decorative qualities. Fortunately for the modern householder wishing to recreate a period rural kitchen, original and reproduction, mass-produced and hand-painted, tiles are available in a wide range of traditional colours, textures, patterns and motifs associated with rural areas and dwellings around the globe.

However, it is important to note certain restrictions on the use of wall tiles in rural settings. Firstly, in many cottages and farmhouses constructed prior to the 20th century the use of tiled splashbacks was often inhibited by the physical properties of the walls themselves. For example, walls made from traditional materials such as wattle and daub and cob, and lime renders and plasters, absorbed water from the ground and outside air and decayed if allowed to become permanently saturated. Unfortunately, ceramic tiles and tile adhesive would have sealed that moisture in, and therefore could not be used. The traditional alternative was to apply several coats of semi-porous limewash or distemper, which minimized the absorption of water and allowed any moisture to evaporate, thereby preserving the substrate of the wall.

Secondly, even in buildings made from brick and stone, wall tiles in most rural kitchens were traditionally confined to the areas immediately behind the sink and draining board, and the stove or range, and even then were only in widespread use by the first two decades of the 20th century. More extensive tiling was very much an urban phenomenon confined, in most ordinary houses, to the late 19th century and beyond.

Above: *Hand-potted tiles make up the splashback behind the sink and drainer in the kitchen of a brick-built Surrey cottage that dates from c.1550. Hand-made, and especially hand-painted tiles are a common feature of country kitchens, and while usually used sparingly in Britain, they are often used extensively in Mediterranean countries.*

Right: *Although these tartan tiles are modern, their design can be traced back to the early 19th century. Tiling behind and around built-in stoves and ranges had become fairly common practice by the beginning of the 20th century.*

Above: *Off-white, glazed ceramic tiles form the splashback behind a double-pot china sink and flanking wooden draining board and work counter. Late 19th- and early 20th-century mass-produced tiles such as these were more often rectangular in shape, rather than square. Reproductions in various colours are widely available.*

Left: *Hand-painted, 18th-century faïence tiles in a Spanish country kitchen.*

Above: *The warm tones and earthy textures of terracotta tiles amply offset the natural chilliness of a tiled surface as compared with, for example, wood. Unglazed tiles can be sealed to make them stain-resistant. If left unglazed they should be scrubbed down on a regular basis for reasons of hygiene.*

Right: *Historically, wall tiles have been used more sparingly in country kitchens than they have in their urban counterparts. Here, however, they have been used extensively to create a deliberately cool recess around the refrigerator.*

Country-Style Floors

When laying down flooring in a country kitchen there is little or no need to compromise period authenticity, as there is with the installation of modern electrical appliances. Traditional materials, such as stone, brick, slate and clay tiles, which have been in common use since Medieval times, provide a practical, durable and hygienic surface rarely bettered by any synthetic or man-made product developed during the latter part of the 20th century.

Traditionally, flagstone floors were cut from locally quarried materials, such as granite, slate and various sandstones. The size of the flags varied, but they were invariably laid square to each other – a rare exception being in a few American Colonial houses, where they were laid diagonally in a chequered pattern. Brick floors, on the other hand, were laid in a variety of patterns, notably herringbone and Flemish-bond, with the brick being set on their edges. Since the latter part of the 19th century, unglazed and glazed terracotta and quarry tiles have been widely used.

Wooden floors were relatively rare in rural kitchens, and largely confined to American Colonial and Federal houses. Pine boards (sometimes bleached or stencilled, but rarely stained or varnished) were typical, although maple and oak were sometimes used in larger houses. The boards were either in random or matching widths, and butt-jointed, half-lapped, tongue-and-grooved or spline-jointed.

To ameliorate the chill of stone, brick and tiled floors, painted floorcloths, rag-strip rugs or rush or coconut matting were often laid on top. Wooden floors were similarly covered, albeit for decorative as much as practical reasons.

Above: *A flagstone floor, with smaller flags forming a contrasting border.*

Left: *Ceramic floor tiles, in slate black with contrasting gray grouting.*

Right: *Coloured stone flags, here laid in a traditional diamond pattern, rather than being offset, or butt-jointed in line.*

Above: *Although it looks like brick, this flooring by Amtico is in fact a high-quality vinyl – and just as durable as the real thing.*

Right: *A flagstone floor; the flags are of variable size as was often the case with stone floors laid in country areas from Medieval times onward.*

Above: *Large stone slabs provide hard-wearing floor-ing in front of the cast-iron* *range, sink and walkway from the kitchen door to the window. In the area set* *aside for eating, however, plain wooden boards are use, as they are both warmer* *underfoot, and "visually" warmer, and more conducive to a dining area.*

Country-Style Stoves and Appliances

Most 19th-century cast-iron, wood- and coal-burning stoves were extremely inefficient and labour-intensive compared to their electric- and gas-powered modern counterparts – although a few of the enclosed ranges produced during the latter part of the century were remarkably sophisticated (see the Introduction, pages 8–17). However, few have survived, and even if one can be obtained from a specialist supplier, they are only an option nowadays for the most adventurous and confident of cooks intent on the most scrupulously accurate of period restorations.

A far more practical option are the 20th-century equivalents such as the Aga or Rayburn. While early versions of these stove-enamelled, cast-iron ranges ran on solid fuel, more recent models are powered by gas, oil or electricity and, as a result, provide the even temperatures necessary for consistent cooking. They are available in various sizes, with different combinations of ovens and hotplates, and they can also provide additional heat for the rest of the kitchen or central heating for the rest of the house.

The heavy-duty steel or cast-iron freestanding stoves, originally designed for professional cooks, are suitable alternatives to stove-enamelled ranges. They incorporate a host of time-saving and safety features, such as flat-top burners, thermostat controls and a combination of gas and electric burners and ovens.

Less expensive alternatives are the modern, freestanding gas or electric cookers, or built-in ovens with separate hobs/cooktops, that incorporate features such as oval glass viewing panels and brass hanging rails and hinges that make them visually more suited to a rural kitchen.

Similarly, most manufacturers offer electrical appliances, such as refrigerators, freezers, dishwashers and microwaves, that can either be built into cupboards/cabinets, or faced with decorative wooden or painted panels, thereby disguising them within a "period" country setting.

Left: *This freestanding pine armoire has been designed to house a large refrigerator and freezer. With the doors shut it would be difficult to distinguish it from a 19th-century example simply used for storage.*

Above: *While many domestic appliances come with decor panels that can be changed to match the material and colour of surrounding cabinets, simply inserting them in a recess, as here, can also render them unobtrusive.*

Above: *A cream-enamelled, Rayburn range. Solid fuel is fetched and carried in the aluminium scuttle.*

Below left: *An early 20th-century, blackleaded, cast-iron range, with double oven and single hotplate.*

Below right: *A top-of-the-range, black and cream-enamelled, four-oven Aga. Highly efficient, gas-*

powered models are now available as an alternative to oil and the original solid fuel examples.

Left: *A 1930s freestanding, vitreous-enamelled, American gas cooker. It incorporates a large and a small oven, both thermostatically controlled, a four-ring hob/cooktop, an overhead pot rack and a built-in splashback. This model has been restored to its original condition. Because gas is potentially explosive, it is strongly advised that anyone wishing to install a period gas cooker has it professionally serviced before use, and any worn parts replaced.*

Above: *A built-in, electric oven with a four-ring gas hob/cooktop above.*

Right: *A built-in dishwasher with a panelled wooden door decor panel.*

Left: *No attempt has been made to disguise this large, freestanding, modern gas cooker, which sits perfectly happily in an American Colonial-style kitchen. Very few householders would wish to replicate the labour-intensive, open-hearth cookery of an original Colonial kitchen, and forsake the advantages of a clean, reliable and controllable source of heat, and an insulated, self-cleaning oven.*

Right: *There are two hobs/cooktops in this kitchen: an electric one built into the work surface of an island; and a gas one built into a run of solid oak storage cupboards/cabinets that have, in turn, been installed in an old inglenook fireplace.*

Country-Style Accessories

Numerous period kitchen accessories can be obtained from antique shops, auctions, thrift shops, jumble and boot sales. They provide an effective means of creating a period look – particularly in country kitchens, where much of the *batterie de cuisine* is permanently on display.

Typical storage items include: stoneware jars; wooden tea caddies; cast-iron pot stands and wicker baskets. For preparing food there are: carved wooden spoons, bread boards, butter stamps and biscuit moulds; salt-glazed and copper jelly moulds; wooden and metal graters; ironstone and enamelled measures; iron pastry wheels, and pestles and mortars.

For cooking and serving there are: cast-iron trivets, pots and skillets; brass and copper preserving pans, and brass, iron and pewter ladles. Other sundry items include: cast-iron apple peelers and corers; wooden coffee mills; brass or cast-iron scales; brass and copper kettles.

Left: A wooden-framed slate pad and a carved candle box, both 19th century, hang on the wall behind a wicker basket containing fruit and a pottery bowl housing a selection of bone-handled knives.

Above: *A dairymaid's wooden yoke has been utilized to provide an ingenious alternative to the typical hanging rack suspended from the ceiling. A variety of wicker baskets store herbs, vegetables and other fruits of the field and garden. On the wall behind, hanging shelves display preserves, jams and other condiments – adjacent to a steel whisk, a toasting fork and a wooden spatula.*

Right: *Ranged on the draining board, tongue-and-groove wall panelling and open shelves to the left of the sink are copper kettles, a decorative copper serving tray, enamelled flour and bread bins and a large mesh food cover. An enamelled colander sits on the work surface to the right of the sink. Nineteenth and early-20th-century kitchenalia such as this often appears in job-lots at auctions, and can be bought reasonably cheaply.*

Above: *A French wire colander, here used to rinse and drain mushrooms and keep them fresh.*

Right: *Ranged on the wall behind the cooker is a collection of cast-iron pastry and biscuit moulds, steel graters, a carved wooden pastry wheel and a cast-iron skillet. Flanked by wicker baskets and storage jars containing a collection of wooden spoons and various wooden-handle knives, are an early 20th-century expresso maker, and wooden-handle copper kettle and an iron jelly mould.*

Above: *Early 20th-century cast-iron spring balance scales, with an enamelled flour bin and steel whisk.*

Above: *A hand-painted duck coat rack, used here to hang a collection of copper ladles, spoons and spatulas.*

Above: *Traditional carved and painted wooden love spoons, displayed in a wall-hung rack.*

Urban-Style Kitchens

As with country kitchens, any modern reproduction of a period urban kitchen will inevitably be a pastiche rather than an exact copy of an original if modern standards of hygiene and convenience are not to be compromised. For example, very few people would wish to install a meat safe and exclude a refrigerator on the grounds of period authenticity. Consequently, the most sensible compromise is to install as many modern appliances as are needed, but to accommodate them into a period-style setting.

Fortunately, there are many specialist kitchen manufacturers and designers in business today who make kitchen furniture in a wide range of traditional urban styles. In many respects this has been a result of the post-Modernist reaction to the Modernism that largely prevailed from the 1920s through to the 1960s and 1970s. More specifically, in terms of kitchen design, there has been a reaction to the uniform, streamlined, built-in, melamine-faced chipboard kitchen, and a revival of various historical styles and traditional standards of craftsmanship. One of the joys of post-Modernism is that it draws on a wide variety of sources for inspiration. It is possible to have custom-made kitchens that replicate the styles of cabinet-making found in Georgian, Victorian and Edwardian urban houses.

A number of companies produce Arts and Crafts-style kitchens inspired by late 19th-century examples. Similarly, Art Nouveau, Art Deco, Santa Fé, neo-Classical and Gothic-revival styles of decoration and ornamentation are also available. Perhaps most ingenious of all, however, is the adaptation of Shaker-style furniture and joinery: traditionally associated with the 18th and 19th century religious communities of rural America, its simple, functional lines and painted surfaces sit quite happily with modern appliances in an urban setting.

Above: *A Santa Fé-style kitchen in natural ash, incorporating carved wooden motifs, such as the sunburst on the extractor hood, redolent of Art Deco. The suspended rack is of steamed ash and wrought iron.*

Left: *A painted wooden, Shaker-style kitchen incorporating a large cooking range with electric double oven and gas hobs/cooktops.*

Above: *The decorative detailing employed in this Sante Fé-style kitchen (also shown below) even extends to the kickboards below the base cabinets.*

Right: *An Arts and Crafts-style London kitchen.*

Below: *Built-in cabinets, peg rails, and hanging shelves feature in this Shaker-style kitchen.*

Right: *The kitchen in Charles Jencks's "Thematic House" in London. At the forefront of post-Modernism, Jencks's work was driven by a reaction to the minimalism and "design straitjacket" of Modernism. This can be seen here in the introduction of various Classical details, such as the pillars at the corners of cabinets – they are, however, employed ironically and in defiance of most of the laws of proportion and structure.*

Below: *The inspiration for this Santa Fé-style kitchen – also shown on the previous page – lies in the architectural styles, patterns and motifs, associated with the Aztec and Inca civilizations of South America.*

Above: *A Biedermeier buffet that has been ingeniously adapted to accommodate a kitchen sink and a hob/cooktop.*

Above: *A built-in kitchen by Smallbone,
featuring a central island with a tiled
work surface, an inset sink and drawers
and a wine rack below. On the right is a
"chicken coup" seat – a throwback to
previous centuries when various livestock were kept in the kitchen. All the
cabinets are made of bleached oak.*

Left: *A modern urban kitchen, with
built-in cabinets cut and carved from
maple. Much of the decorative detailing
is Etruscan-inspired – notably the cornice, pilasters and drawer and cabinet
handles/pulls. The contrast between
black and white (or other pale colours)
that is typical of the style, is found here
in the juxtaposition of the black marble
work counter, oven and hob/cooktop,
and the pale beech cabinets.*

Urban-Style Painted Kitchens

One of the main distinctions, especially since the the late-18th century, between the urban and country kitchen, has been the greater use of built-in kitchen cupboards/cabinets in the former, as against more freestanding items of furniture in the latter. Traditionally the majority of urban built-in cupboards/cabinets were painted, rather than simply stained and polished or varnished.

Up until the end of the 19th century, most urban kitchen cabinets were flat-painted. For example, in early Georgian kitchens the plain but elegant ranks of drawers and cupboards in housekeeper's rooms were usually painted in drab, a grayish or dull-brown colour. In late Georgian kitchens, drab remained popular, although sage green became an increasingly common alternative. On the other side of the Atlantic, North American Federal and Empire-style kitchens often featured built-in pine cupboards painted in dark red or various shades of green.

By the second half of the 19th century, there was an increasing use of off-white and cream-coloured paint – a development that, together with improved lighting, made the basement and semi-basement kitchens of many urban Victorian houses less gloomy to work in. Right at the end of the century, many Art Nouveau-style kitchens incorporated wooden cupboards/cabinets painted white and featuring doors decorated with stencilled motifs and purple glass. Darker colours also remained popular – a mid-to-dark green often being used in Arts and Crafts-style kitchens.

While paler colours have tended to predominate for much of the 20th century, in recent years many kitchen designers and manufacturers have begun to replicate the period painted urban look by using a range of paint techniques, such as dragging, colourwashing, ragging and antiquing. The antiquing technique, for instance, produces a finish that simulates the effects of general wear and tear, as well as a soft patina of age. Paint finishes are enjoying a renaissance and they provide lots of subtle and exciting ways of applying paint (see the period finishes on pages 106–112).

Above: *The wall panelling and doors of this urban kitchen have been dragged and frottaged to produce a simple, fantasy woodgrain effect. (Frottage is the technique of dabbing wet paint with a rag, sponge or cellophane to produce irregular markings and patterns.)*

Right: *A pastiche of an early Edwardian kitchen, with painted wooden cupboards and modern appliances.*

Above: *A built-in pine dresser in the kitchen of a Huguenot house in Spitalfields, London. Because the dresser has* *been painted in the same traditional cream colour as the wall panelling, it appears less obtrusive than if it were simply polished.*

Above: *These built-in cabinets are made from tulipwood, and feature glazed Gothic-arched doors on either side of the cream and black enamelled Aga. The wood has been painted in blue and gold with a distressed finish.*

Left: *The classical detailing of this idealized version of a Georgian urban kitchen extends from the Palladian window to the pilasters on the corners of the cabinets, the dentil mouldings in the cornice above the wall cabinets, and the flagstone floor. The 20th-century Aga is an evolutionary descendant of the original cast-iron range, designed by Thomas Robinson in 1780.*

Above: *A painted wooden kitchen in the basement of a terraced town house. In addition to installing effective general and task lighting, it is invariably a* sensible idea to use white or pale colours in "below stairs" kitchens, which can otherwise be rather gloomy, given the minimal amount of natural daylight present.

Above: *A Shaker-style kitchen with hand-painted wooden cabinets and dresser and a beech work surface. The clean lines of traditional Shaker furniture lend themselves perfectly to the functional and decorative requirements of the modern urban kitchen, and enjoy a happy alliance with stream-lined, modern appliances. The peg rack on the wall above the cabinets is a common feature in Shaker houses, and is ideal for hanging kitchen utensils, and even herbs and vegetables, close to where they are needed.*

Left: *The washing-up area of this kitchen incorporates a glazed cast-iron sink set into a marble worktop/counter, brass swan-neck mixer taps/ faucets, hand-painted tiles and painted wooden cabinets with Gothic-style arches on the doors.*

Right: *The combination of glass-fronted wall cabinets, open shelving, a wine rack and drawers of various sizes – all painted – give this large urban kitchen the look of a late 19th- or early 20th-century butler's pantry*

Below: *This "Hand-Painted Pilaster Kitchen" by Smallbone draws its inspiration from the 18th century, and in particular classical decorative details such as gently tapering half columns (pilasters), cornices, mouldings and raised and fielded panels. The built-in cabinets have been painted ivory; the freestanding dresser in a rich viridian colourwash.*

Left: *A modern reproduction of the sort of kitchen found in many larger urban households during the early part of the 20th century (although the Aga is slightly later than that). The wooden cabinets are pine, and distressed with paint to create the appearance of age. The strap hinges on the cabinets and the drop handles/pulls on the doors are solid brass. The work surface is mahogany, and the brass mixer tap/faucet is lever-operated with ceramic handles.*

Right: *A kitchen in an Edwardian townhouse. The wooden cupboards/cabinets were painted in two shades of cream, rubbed back with sandpaper, and then treated with a little burnt umber to artificially age them. They were then sealed with varnish to protect them from moisture and general wear and tear, and also make them easier to clean. A central pine table and Windsor-style chairs provide a large dining facility, and the table top also doubles up as a surface for the preparation of food.*

Above: *A hand-painted kitchen, with classically-inspired decorative details, installed in a conservatory. The built-in base cabinets have been colourwashed in contrasting shades of green. The open plate rack is painted a putty colour, which ties it in to the white-glazed earthenware sink below.*

Left: *The subtle gradations of colour in this kitchen are created by distressing semi-translucent pink glazes over a contrasting coloured (off-white) ground coat. The work surface and sink is synthetic marble.*

Urban-Style Furniture

In addition to floor and wall-mounted built-in cupboards/cabinets, the urban kitchen of previous centuries has been traditionally furnished with a variety of freestanding items of furniture, used for either storage or a range of tasks relating to the preparation of food. Yet for much of this century freestanding pieces have tended to be omitted in favour of a streamlined, "fitted" look. Recently, however, this trend has been reversed as designers and manufacturers come to realise that, provided there is sufficient space available, pieces of freestanding furniture can be extremely versatile and ergonomically efficient, especially when used in combination with built-in cabinets.

In larger kitchens, the dresser has made a come back, and is available in virtually any period style. Whatever the style, in urban kitchens dressers are invariably painted and have top cupboards/cabinets, usually with glazed doors and often central open shelving.

Other pieces that have made a comeback in recent years are: larder cupboards, often with ventilated doors to ensure a circulation of fresh air around perishable commodities; butcher's block tables, which are usually on castors and can be moved around. Central islands, work benches or tables, often fitted with multi-surface worktops/counters, are also popular.

Above: *This freestanding food cupboard provides a practical alternative to a built-in larder. Made of ash, it incorporates sliding willow baskets for storing vegetables, deep drawers for cans and suchlike, and a large, ventilated top cupboard with deep shelves for dried, bottled and packaged food.*

Above: *A lacquered oak worktable, with a ladder back for hanging kitchen utensils conveniently close to hand. One half of the work counter is granite which provides a cool surface for preparing pastry.*

Left: *A central island, painted green and with a combined synthetic and natural ash work surface.*

Above left: *A wall-mounted plate rack, incorporating top cupboards/cabinets. Made of natural ash, it is embellished with decorative details, such as a stepped moulding on the cornice, associated with the South-American-influenced Santa Fé style.*

Above right: *A large, freestanding, enclosed dresser, by Smallbone. The top cupboards/cabinets feature acid-etched, chequerboard glass in the doors, while the doors at the bottom are embellished with inlay.*

Left: *A Shaker-style, two-part dresser, with open shelving flanked by cup-boards/cabinets with glazed doors on the top section. The combination of cupboards/cabinets, drawers (of various sizes) and shelves makes the dresser very versatile when it comes to storage. Although Shaker communities in the United States have always been predominantly based in the countryside, the clean lines and functional simplicity of their style of furniture makes it well-suited to urban kitchens of the late 20th century.*

Right: *A mahogany-stained Shaker cupboard/cabinet, c.1870. The child's high-chair is slightly older. The chair rails for hanging chairs on the walls were a common feature of Shaker kitchens, and provided an ideal way of increasing the available floor space once meals had been completed.*

Below: *A large, freestanding dresser, hand-painted in green and red. Stylized turned and carved tulips support the cornice, which features a dentil moulding. The open shelving, designed to store and display crockery, has a shaped and pierced frieze. (The three-tiered sliding divisions within the central drawer section are shown on page 71, bottom right.)*

Right: *A Victorian, wrought and cast-iron buffet trolley, with marble top, castors and brass embellishments.*

Left: *A small and rather plain side table, painted to blend in with the wall panelling, in the corner of the kitchen in a Georgian townhouse in Spitalfields, London.*

Above: *An enclosed dresser, showing classical detailing in the use of slim pilasters, a dentilled cornice, and the raised and fielded panels on the lower cupboard/cabinet doors. The use of glass in the cupboard/cabinet doors, makes this dresser better suited to an urban rather than a rural kitchen – as does the distressed blue paint finish.*

Right: *A breakfront wooden dresser, painted in two shades of cream, rubbed back, and artificially aged with a little burnt umber artist's oil.*

DINING FURNITURE

Prior to the 20th century, eating meals in the majority of urban kitchens was largely the preserve of servants; the householders would have taken their meals in a separate parlour or dining room. However, during the latter part of the 19th century, as kitchens became warmer, less humid, better lit, and generally more pleasant as a working environment, householders began to take some of their meals at the kitchen table.

A general reduction in the size of townhouses and an increase in the number of flats and apartments during the 1920s and 1930s further fuelled the integration of the kitchen and the dining room.

In the United States, the development of breakfast bars, usually in the form of an extended work surface, and often on a central island, allowed snack meals to be eaten, sitting on high-stools, where there was not sufficient space for a table and chairs – an idea that soon caught on in Britain and Europe, especially in houses and apartments that were designed by architects of the Modern Movement.

Where space was not a problem, tables and chairs were usually positioned in a clearly defined dining area of the eat-in kitchen. The style of the table invariably reflected the style of furniture and joinery in the kitchen area. Thus, traditional formal dining tables, in hardwoods such as mahogany, oak and beech, and with matching sets of chairs (rather than with "mixed" sets, as was often the case in country areas), tended to be installed where grander and more elaborately ornamented cupboards and other kitchen cabinets had been chosen, or where there was a floor constructed from the same wood. Similarly, painted tables (usually made of a softwood such as pine) tended to be colour-matched to painted cupboards/cabinets.

Above: *A dining table and chairs from Charles Jencks's post-Modern "Thematic House". One of the advantages for householders wishing to install a new kitchen in the post-Modern era is that anything goes. Here Greek Classical, Egyptian, Art Nouveau and Art Deco patterns and motifs have all been combined to create a style all of its own.*

Left: *The central island in an Italian kitchen provides not only a work surface for preparing food, but also a table for eating informal meals at. Because the wooden work surface overlaps the cupboards/cabinets below, the rush-seated stools can be stored without unduly encroaching into the rest of the kitchen.*

Left: *In this modern reproduction of a painted Edwardian kitchen, a pine refectory table and matching chairs provide an ample dining space for a large family. The pine has been artificially aged with an antiquing glaze.*

Below: *A maple-topped dining table, supported on a beech frame, and equipped with two drawers – useful for storing cutlery, kitchen utensils and table napkins. The five stickback chairs, made of oak, are supplemented with a pair of bentwood chairs.*

Left: *Shaker-style, drop-leaf dining table and (reproduction) 18th-century ladder-back chairs. The chair seats, painted blue like the table, are woven from thin strips of wood.*

Above: *Contrasting coloured woods for the kitchen cabinets and the dining table, plus formal, leather-backed chairs, clearly distinguish the kitchen and dining areas of this eat-in kitchen.*

Urban-Style Storage

Apart from the freestanding pieces of furniture referred to on pages 64–7, much of the storage in urban kitchens since the Georgian era has been built-in or fitted. For instance, the aumbrey (a cupboard installed in a recess or niche in the wall) has remained in use, if not in name, since Medieval times. By the middle of the 18th century, housekeeper's rooms adjoining the kitchen were fitted out with drawers and shelves; by the end of the century, utilitarian china cupboards and built-in shelving had become standard even in the most modest of urban kitchens.

It was during the late 19th century that the fitted kitchen began to slowly emerge. The advent of mechanized joinery resulted in a reduction of the cost of furniture in general, and in the kitchen led to built-in dressers and, more significantly, the transformation of much open shelving in kitchens and pantries into wall cabinets.

The early fitted look is best seen in some of the British Arts and Crafts and American Beaux Arts inspired kitchens designed during the 1880s and 1890s: their shelves, cabinets and work surfaces pre-empted the 20th century built-in kitchen.

Above: *Built-in, painted wooden plate racks and open shelves above and to the side of the draining board provide an ideal means of storing and displaying hand-painted plates, bowls and other items of crockery close to the sink.*

Right: *By incorporating shelves in the doors of this walk-in larder or pantry, the storage space is maximized. Unlike enclosed drawers, the sliding wicker baskets allow air to circulate around their contents, and are thus ideal for storing perishables, such as fruit and vegetables.*

Right: *A Shaker peg rail, here used to support painted hanging shelves and a pair of reproduction 18th-century, ladder-back dining chairs with painted, woven wooden seats. The peg rack offers a most versatile and efficient means of storage in the kitchen, especially where space is restricted.*

Above: *Above a solid ash central island with a range of cabinets and drawers, a suspended rack features not only bars for hanging utensils from, but also shelves for storage and display.*

Above: *A large, freestanding pine dresser, with drawers for storage and open shelving above and below. Installed in an urban kitchen/diner, the dresser has been dragged in a semi-translucent reddish-brown oil-based glaze to simulate the appearance of mahogany. To produce an accurate simulation of mahogany graining, see the technique illustrated on pages 98–9.*

Right: *Deep storage for various items of tableware and other crockery is provided by the three-tiered sliding drawers disguised behind a drawer panel of a painted, freestanding dresser. This type of storage layout is designed to make it easier to find items than if they had been stored in conventional drawers. There is also less bending down required to view the contents.*

Urban-Style Work Surfaces

As in period country kitchens, wood has traditionally been used for the majority of work surfaces in urban kitchens. A large wooden table, usually centrally placed if space allows, doubles up for the preparation and eating of meals. If there is no room for a central work table, free-standing butcher's block tables, incorporating a durable hardwood top designed for cutting and chopping ingredients, are a very useful substitute.

In terms of work surfaces, the main difference between rural and urban kitchens is the fact that there has been a much more extensive use of materials such as marble, slate, granite, ceramic tiles and, during the latter part of the 20th century, brushed and stainless steel in urban settings. They have also tended to be employed in long, unbroken runs of one level – whereas in country kitchens worktops/counters, like the storage cabinets beneath them, have often been separated out, and sometimes at different heights.

Work surfaces made from tiles or stone are durable, easy to clean and hygienic. This is true of tiles since the advent of epoxy-resin grout/caulk (first developed for hospitals) which includes substances that inhibit the growth of mould and other agents that can cause infections.

Although these surfaces are, to varying degrees, cold to the touch compared with wood, this does have its advantages for certain aspects of food preparation. Moreover, they are available in a range of colours that helps to offset this coldness and means that they can be co-ordinated with other decorative elements in the kitchen. For example, marble comes in a variety of subtle colourings and attractive veining patterns, and granite is available in hues of gray, brown and pink, broken up with masses of tiny dots of colour. Of course, modern materials are also available and are made to simulate marble, granite and other natural surfaces.

Above: *Plain white ceramic tiles, finished off with a lacquered pine fillet along the leading edge, provide most of the work surface in this urban kitchen.* *However, a large, hardwood chopping block has been inset on top of one of the cupboards, and provides a durable surface for chopping meat, herbs and vegetables.*

Right: *A variety of work surfaces have been installed in this kitchen. On either side of the sink grooved teak stands up to the rigours of constant soaking and drying out. In the far corner, slabs of granite have been used, their natural chilliness making them ideal for rolling out pastry. On the central island, beech – sensibly set at different heights for different tasks – makes up the majority of the work surface, and is well-suited to chopping up meat, herbs and vegetables.*

Below: *Detail of a gray granite work surface – showing the fossiliferous forms that make it such an attractive surface to work with.*

Left: *Granite work surfaces are generally less expensive than marble ones, but just as durable. If desired – as here – they are capable of taking a high polish.*

Above: *Ceramic tiles also make a very durable work surface, although like marble and granite, they are unforgiving if crockery or glass is dropped on them.*

Urban-Style Sinks and Taps

As with country kitchens (see pages 42–3), the most authentic sink for the period urban kitchen remains a reproduction or an original glazed stoneware or white porcelain-enamelled fireclay sink. White enamelled cast-iron and marble sinks are equally suitable. Stainless steel sinks, however, are more appropriate for houses and apartments built from the 1930s onward.

Butler sinks in urban settings can be supported on brick piers or corbels, or cast-iron brackets. However, in recent years this type of sink has more commonly been mounted on top of a base cabinet, with its rim set just below the level of the surrounding and slightly overlapping draining board/work surface. In other words, the fashion in urban kitchens was to build it in, rather than leave it freestanding.

As already discussed (again, see pages 42–3), the advantage most of these traditional butler sinks have over many modern counterparts lies in the greater width and depth of their bowl(s).

However, working for any length of time at a sink more than approximately 15cm/6in deep will, when it is set below the level of the surrounding drainer/work surface, result in backache. If you intend to purchase an original rather than a reproduction model, do not be palmed off with an industrial laboratory sink. It may look like traditional domestic butler sink, but its greater depth will soon cause discomfort.

As in country kitchens, the spoke- or cross-shaped, capstan-topped tap/faucet that was in general use up until the 1920s and 1930s was eventually superseded in many urban kitchens by single-spout mixer taps, many of which were lever-operated. While the solid brass and brass-finish taps, best associated with rural kitchens are not totally out of place in urban settings reproduction or original porcelain-enamelled chromium-plated, nickel-silver-plated, gun metal and, in post 1930s houses, stainless steel examples remain more in keeping.

Above: *A chrome mixer tap/faucet with capstan handles.*

Right: *A combined, stainless brushed steel sink and drainer/work surface. The tap/faucet delivers cold water only – the sink having been designed purely for washing and preparing vegetables and other ingredients close to the stove.*

Above: *A monobloc brass tap/faucet with capstan handles, designed for mounting on the work surface or sink.*

Above: *A shelf sink, with built-in overflow and a ledge designed for either pillar taps/faucets or bibcocks with upstands. The grooved drainer is made of granite.*

Right: *An inset enamelled cast-iron sink, supplied by a brass mixer tap/faucet, mounted at the back of a polished granite drainer/ work surface.*

Above: *An inset china clay sink, with overflow, grooved and canted wooden draining boards, and a lever-operated mixer tap/faucet.*

Right: *A china clay sink, inset into a Palladian style cabinet with applied Corinthian pilasters and fielded panels. The wall-mounted brass mixer tap/faucet behind is lever-operated.*

Urban-Style Tiles

Generally speaking, tiles were used to protect and decorate the walls of kitchens and their ancillary rooms from an earlier date and on a more extensive scale in urban houses than they were in rural dwellings. For example, delftware tile picture panels, depicting stylized river scenes, were installed in the pantry of the dwelling house attached to Lambeth Distillery in about 1800.

While such intricately patterned (and costly) tiles, particularly when applied over an entire wall, were the exception rather than the rule, the majority of 19th-century urban kitchens did incorporate simple tiled splashbacks behind sinks and drainers and, to a lesser extent, stoves and ranges. Plain colours predominated, although geometric patterns were also popular.

It was only toward the end of the 19th century that tiles began to spread beyond the splashback along the walls behind other work surfaces – a practice that has endured in urban kitchens throughout the 20th century. For example, in many North American Beaux Arts houses built between 1870–1920 extensive runs of glazed tiles were used, some embellished with intricate patterns such as delicate festoons containing garlands of flowers, ribbons and bows. Similarly, tiled dados were installed in numerous British late-Victorian and Edwardian kitchens.

For anyone wishing to recreate a period-style kitchen, a wide range of 19th and 20th century reproduction tiles in authentic period colours and patterns are available.

Above: Hand-painted tiles provide an attractive, durable and easy-to-clean surface on the wall behind this integrated cooking unit.

Left: An industrial style cooking range, in white and with chrome pull handles, is flanked by freestanding cabinets, and backed by an altar-like ceramic tiled splashback that matches the floor tiles and is framed by a contrasting decorative tile frieze.

Left: *In this urban kitchen, plain-coloured ceramic tiles on the work surface have been contrasted with different-coloured, and randomly patterned tiles on the splashback.*

Below: *Glazed hand-made wall tiles line the recess behind a cream and black enamelled Aga. The middle panel of the tiles is laid out in a diamond pattern, which contrasts with the butt-jointed border.*

Above: *Hand-made tiles by the potters Hinchcliffe and Barber provide a work surface to ceiling splashback in the "wet" area of the kitchen. The blue and green colours in the geometric and animal motifs are echoed in painted shelves and base cabinets.*

Right: *Wall tiles provide an easy-to-clean surface around open shelves.*

Urban-Style Floors

In the majority of urban houses built from the Middle Ages up to the latter part of the 19th century, the preferred materials for flooring in the kitchen were stone, brick and various types of tiles, although in the grandest houses marble was sometimes used. As in rural kitchens flagstones tended to be set square to each other while bricks were laid on edge in a variety of traditional patterns. Tiles, notably those made of slate or baked clay, were often either laid in, or decorated with, geometric patterns.

Until the first half of the 19th century, wooden floors were largely confined to North American Colonial and Federal houses. Butt-jointed pine boards were typical in smaller houses, although tongue-and-grooved white pine was often used in larger houses. While most pine floors were bleached, and sometimes stencilled or painted, during the second half of the 19th century a dark stained and polished finish proved increasingly popular, as did polished hardwoods such as oak and maple. Throughout Britain and Europe, wooden floorboards only gradually began to appear at the beginning of the 19th century, and then only in kitchens with suspended wooden sub-floors. As in America, pine was the preferred option, although it was generally stained and polished or varnished, rather than bleached or left untreated. Toward the end of the 19th century woodblock or parquet floors became fashionable on both sides of the Atlantic, and have remained popular ever since.

Practical alternatives to all of the above have included linoleum and various composites, such as Ebernite. Linoleum was introduced c.1860 and remained fashionable up until the Second World War. Made from compressed cork and linseed oil mounted on a stout canvas backing, it came in plain colours and simulations of superior finishes such as parquet or marble. Ebernite, made from a mixture of wood fibre, mineral powder and a cementing liquid proved popular from the turn of the century until the 1930s. Today vinyl floor covering is produced to simulate a wide variety of natural materials – tiles, marble, wood and cork.

Above: *With their subtle textures and gradations of colour, slate tiles make an attractive and durable floor covering.*

Right: *Strip oak flooring, like pine and beech, provides a warmer alternative underfoot to marble, slate and ceramic tiles, and can be co-ordinated with the work surface to provided a contrast with painted cupboards/cabinets.*

Above: *Brick tiles are more usually associated with country kitchens but, as here, make an elegant addition to an "unfitted" urban kitchen.*

Left: *Large white ceramic tiles, laid with contrasting diamond-shaped black inserts, make an elegant floor covering that is better suited to the greater formality of an urban kitchen than a rural one. Floors such as this were often laid in marble during the 18th and 19th centuries.*

Above: *Linoleum dates back to c.1860 and is made from compressed cork and linseed oil fixed to a canvas back.*

Extremely durable, it is available in plain, marbled, wood-grained and, as here, stridently patterned colours.

Above: *Very large slate tiles, in various shades of gray and gray-green make a bold statement in this large*

urban kitchen. The extremely wide grout lines further emphasise the size and contrasting colours of the tiles.

Urban-Style Stoves and Appliances

In recent years it has become fashionable to incorporate a cast-iron Aga or similar range when installing a period-style kitchen in a town house. This trend can partly be explained by the fact that the Aga – the 20th-century successor to the Victorian cast-iron range – has come to be recognised as a classic piece of design which, although originally and almost exclusively installed in country kitchens, sits happily in virtually any location or style of kitchen. Equally, the development of oil, gas and even electric models have made the Aga a more reliable appliance for cooking on, even if it cannot match the efficiency of modern fan-assisted electric ovens and thermostat-controlled gas and electric hobs (cooktops).

However, the main drawback to installing an Aga or a similar cast-iron range in most urban kitchens is its weight: it will be far too heavy for a suspended wooden sub-floor unless it is reinforced below with a combination of brick or concrete piers and reinforced steel girders. As a consequence of this, many urban householders creating a period-style kitchen have installed lighter, freestanding stoves incorporating integrated gas and electric burners and ovens, such as the models designed for professional cooks by commercial manufacturers. Serious home cooks also prefer the larger scale, higher power and robust styling of professional equipment.

However, the technological and space-saving advantages of separate, built-in ovens/drop-in ranges and hobs/cooktops compensate for a lack of strict period authenticity. They can be very effectively harmonized with a traditional urban setting by building them – together with other electrical appliances such as refrigerators, freezers and dishwashers – into authentic period-style cupboards/cabinets and worktops/counters.

Above: *Because they are finished in black, this ceramic hob/cooktop and built-under, fan-assisted, electric oven recall the black-leaded, cast-iron range found at the heart of most kitchens during the 19th century.*

Right: *This maple and granite cooking unit can either be freestanding, or built into a run of other cabinets. It houses a fan-assisted electric oven/drop-in range and an electric ceramic hob/cooktop. The brushed steel fixture above houses an extractor fan which conducts smoke, steam and accompanying cooking smells to outside of the house.*

Above: *A professional cook-ing range, with fan-assisted twin electric ovens, a four-ring gas hob/cooktop and a* large electric warming plate. The drawers underneath the ovens are for storing baking trays and roasting dishes.

Above: *A detail from "The Cook's Kitchen", designed by Mark Wilkinson for restaurateur, Anthony Worral Thompson's home, and showing the large, professional-quality cooking range.*

Left: *In this urban L-shaped kitchen, essential appliances – dishwasher, cooker and refrigerator – are placed along one wall, while the sink and a mixture of enclosed and open cup-boards/cabinets line up along the other. The base cabinets have been painted a near-identical shade of blue-green to the refrigera-tor (which is a modern reproduction of a 1950s model).*

Above: *A hi-tech extractor can be effectively concealed within a period-style housing cabinet, here in solid pine.*

Right: *A black-enamelled kitchen range by Lacanche. Among the numerous features are twin ovens, with storage drawers below, a five ring gas hob/cooktop and a cast-iron griddle plate. The splashback and extractor hood incorporates a bar for hanging pots and pans and other kitchen utensils within easy reach when cooking.*

Above: *An elaborately decorated Continental Art Deco range, made of cast-iron –* bronzed and enamelled – with four ovens and five warming plates.

Above: *A black and cream enamelled, oil-fired Rayburn range, with three ovens and* two warming plates. Cooker such as this sit happily in urban and rural kitchens.

Above: *A black-enamelled Aga, with four ovens and three warming plates.*

Left: *A professional-quality, gas cooker, in brushed stainless steel incorporating twin ovens and grills, and two four-ring hobs/cooktops.*

Below: *No attempt has been made to disguise the modern built-in oven and hob/cook-top in this painted period-style kitchen. Yet, like other modern built-in domestic appliances, it sits quite happily with the "older" elements in the room.*

Urban-Style Accessories

Many kitchen accessories in urban houses were traditionally stored out of sight in drawers and cupboards/cabinets – particularly from the latter part of the 19th century and beyond – whereas in rural kitchens, for the most part, they were stored on open display. Nevertheless, incorporating various items of kitchenalia dating from the 18th, 19th and early 20th centuries in any modern recreation of a period urban kitchen is still one of the most effective means of helping to establish an authentic period look.

Traditionally, the range of kitchen accessories available to the urban dweller was broadly similar to that found in rural households. (For a list of typical items see pages 84–5). However, there were some differences in the style and construction of individual pieces that made them distinctly urban or rural in appearance. This is especially the case with hand-carved wooden items, such as spoons, butter stamps and biscuit moulds, which in rural areas were invariably embellished with rustic patterns and motifs that were not found on their generally plainer urban equivalents.

Similarly, there was a far greater preponderance of items made from newer metals, such as steel, aluminium and, later, chrome, in urban kitchens than there was in rural ones where more traditional, "pre-industrial" materials, such as forged and cast iron and copper, remained the preferred choice.

Another significant difference that began to emerge between urban and rural kitchens during the late 19th century lay in the various types of storage vessels on display. While stoneware jars and wooden caddies remained common to both, an ever-greater number of decorative tins and boxes bearing the maker's name and content appeared on the open shelves and in the glass-fronted cabinets of urban kitchens. A product of the advertising industry, they initially found most of their market among the larger and generally more affluent urban populations of the time.

Above: *This chrome pasta maker would make a stylish addition to any urban kitchen, regardless of period*

Left: *A wall-mounted Santa Fé-style wooden rack for* storing and displaying bat-terie de cuisine *and various herbs, vegetables and other ingredients.*

Left: *An assortment of copper pots and pans and steel sieves and colanders hang from a suspended brass rack over the range.*

Above: *A collection of hand-painted china and tole trays are wall-hung for display purposes only behind the 1950s gas cooker.*

Above: *A stylish Dualit toaster, finished in chrome. Originally designed for use in professional kitchens, it now enjoys domestic use.*

Left: *A chrome and glass juicer. This is a modern reproduction of a design originated in the 1940s.*

Above: *Cotton napkins and glasscloths or tea towels hang on a pole beneath the kitchen mantel shelf. On the*

mantel shelf itself and on the chimney breast is a collection of blue and white china.

KITCHEN
PRACTICALITIES

Planning your Kitchen

Regardless of period or style, when planning the layout of a kitchen it is important to take into account the relationship between the different task areas or work zones, and decide how they should be positioned in relation to one another to achieve the most ergonomically efficient arrangement possible.

In their book on kitchen planning, *Spaces in the Home: Kitchens and Laundering Spaces*, The Department of the Environment recommend an ideal arrangement for positioning appliances, cupboards/cabinets and work surfaces, which is based on a "work triangle" that takes into account storage, food preparation and cooking areas or zones (for a more detailed examination of zones, see the following pages).

In all of the diagrams shown opposite, storage is represented by a refrigerator, food preparation by the sink and cooking by a hob/cooktop. When the three elements are connected up by an imaginary triangle, the Department of the Environment recommend that the total length of the three sides of the triangle should ideally be no less than 3.6m/11ft 10in and no more than 6.6m/21ft 8in, in order to allow for sufficient space for close-to-hand storage, as well as for safety, economy and efficiency.

The safety factor in the kitchen is of paramount importance, and further advice is given on pages 90–1. In the context of the work triangle, safety is compromised if heavy pots and pans have to be moved too far from one zone, such as for food preparation, to another, such as for cooking. This is exacerbated if the pot or pan contains hot or boiling liquids. Consequently, it is recommended that there should be no doors – internal or external – within the area defined by the work triangle. If there are, it increases the

Considerable thought has gone into this Art Deco-inspired kitchen, which features solid maple cabinets with a combination of coloured sycamore veneers. In a U-shape, it has clearly defined work zones: the hob/cooktop sits at the centre of an altarpiece of cupboards/cabinets, which house cooking ingredients, as well as an extractor unit, a food mixer and a toaster. The washing-up zone has a triple-pot sink, below a rack for hanging pots and pans. The oven is conveniently close to large areas of granite work surface, allowing dishes and pans to be taken out and put down quickly. The central island serves as a food preparation and eating area, and is augmented with an octagonal breakfast bar at the entrance to the kitchen.

risk of accidentally banging into someone suddenly entering the kitchen. If the shape of the room is such that there is no way to avoid a door being within the work triangle, then at the very least the appliances and storage cupboards/cabinets should be installed so that the door does not cross the route from the cooker to the sink.

For safety and efficiency the Department of the Environment also recommend that "food preparation, dish washing and cooking zones should be part of the same continuous run of fitments but, provided they are within easy reach of the sink and cooker and are complete in themselves, the zones for food storage and mixing may be separate".

Broadly speaking, there are five basic shapes in which to plan a kitchen, and the choice will largely be determined by the size and shape of the room. A galley kitchen (shown in the diagram top right) consists of cupboards/cabinets and appliances sited on opposite walls. An in-line kitchen (not shown) is ranged along one wall. A U-shape kitchen (shown middle right) has the cupboards and appliances on three walls, and is the most versatile when it comes to establishing an efficient work triangle. An L-shaped kitchen (shown bottom right) has its cupboards/cabinets and appliances along two adjacent walls, which do not have to be the same length. An island kitchen (also shown middle right) has cupboards/cabinets and appliances on either two or three walls, together with an "island" unit in the centre. This unit can either consist of a work surface mounted on storage cupboards/cabinets, or also incorporate an extra sink and or hob/cooktop and have its work surface divided into sections of different heights and materials, as in the example shown opposite left.

It is also important to bear in mind that the recommended minimum clearance between cupboards and appliances on opposite walls is 120cm/4ft. However, if it is extremely unlikely that more than one person will use the kitchen at any one time, plus if there is no throughway between doors, this clearance could be reduced to 100cm/3ft 3in – but not if a low-level built-in oven has been installed. When planning a kitchen remember to use common sense. For instance, the more frequently an item is used the more accessible it should be and try to make work areas as adaptable as possible so as to make the most of the space available.

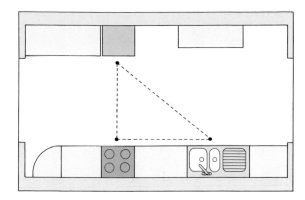

Above: *A work triangle in a galley kitchen, in which the hob/cooktop and sink are sited along one wall, and the refrigerator is positioned on the opposite wall.*

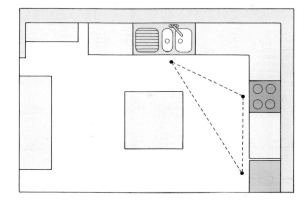

Above: *A U-shaped kitchen in which the work triangle is established on adjacent sides, and is augmented, but not obstructed, by a large, central island.*

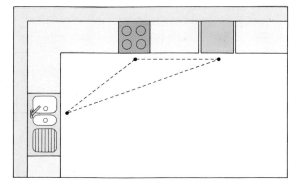

Above: *An L-shaped layout, this time with the hob/cooktop and refrigerator in along one wall, and the sink on the other. Provided there is sufficient space, an L- shape kitchen such as this can accommodate a dining table (in the bottom right-hand corner), as it in no way obstructs the work triangle.*

Safety and Ventilation

Safety is not an optional extra in the kitchen. Statistically more accidents happen here than in any other room in the house. Fortunately, accidents can be avoided if sufficient thought is given to planning the kitchen, and due care and attention is exercised when working in it.

In the diagram, opposite, attention is drawn to typical danger areas, and it should be studied with the following advice on safety.

1 Store frequently used items such as teapots, tea, coffee, sugar, salt and pepper, immediately above the area you normally use them. This will minimize the amount of stretching, bending or twisting you have to do.

2 Store regularly used china as close to the sink and dishwasher as possible. Open plate racks provide an efficient and less arduous means of storage than a closed cupboard/cabinet in which heavy plates are stacked on top of one another.

3 Do not install wall cabinets with hinged doors wider than 50cm/20in. If left open they can cause injuries to eyes, face and head.

4 Make sure that electrical sockets are installed above the work surface as close to where the appliance they are intended for normally stands;

and at a height at which they can be reached over the top of the appliance. Shorten all appliance leads so that there are no long loops of cable lying around.

5 Some of the worst accidents are caused by young children reaching up and grabbing pans and pulling them down on top of themselves. Make sure you leave all pan handles facing away from the front edge of the hob/cooktop, but preferably buy an adjustable guard, and fit it around the perimeter of the hob/cooktop.

Avoid electric hobs/cooktops with coiled elements. Statistically, these are the largest single cause of fires in the kitchen; primarily because they can reach temperatures at which many items instantly combust, rather than start to smoulder if accidentally dropped on them.

Gas hobs/cooktops have a favourable record in relation to kitchen fires, although you should never hang tea towels or clothing to dry above them (this applies to all types of hob/cooktop). The danger with gas hobs/cooktops arises if there is a lack of proper ventilation in the kitchen. You must ensure that there is a permanent supply of fresh air (see the diagram below left), otherwise

Above: *A supply of fresh air, achieved via a combination of air-bricks and extractor fans, is necessary for the safe and efficient combustion of gas hobs/cooktops, and the removal of steam and cooking odours.*

Right: *Good ventilation is also required in cabinets used to store perishable commodities, such as fruit and vegetables. Here, a combination of wooden grills and open-top sliding baskets have been used to that end.*

a burner on a low setting could be blown out if say a door was quickly closed. The subsequent build up of gas might result in an explosion. (Fortu-nately, many manufacturers are making gas hobs with flame failure safety devices.)

Install a work surface between 30–45cm/12–18in in length on either side of the hob/cooktop, so that pots and pans can be removed from the heat and quickly and safely put down.

6 Store regularly used pots and pans as close to the hob as possible, as on the rack here, so you do not have to overly stretch or bend for them.

7 Use the space immediately above the worktop to keep items such as chopping blocks close to hand. Hang them on hooks, or free-stand them against the splashback.

8 Consider installing lever taps/faucets, rather than the capstan sort, if any member of the household suffers from arthritis or a similar complaint. These can be turned on and off with the side of a hand or an elbow. Also, make sure that the water supply to the cold tap /faucet comes direct from the mains (and is therefore fit for drinking) rather than from technically stagnant water in a storage tank in the loft – in most countries, the latter connection is illegal.

9 Choose a large sink, but avoid one that is too deep. If it is deeper than 17cm/7in anyone working at it for any length of time will develop backache. Preferably choose one with a double bowl, as it is very useful for washing and rinsing.

10 Keep kitchen knives sharp at all times: you are more likely to cut yourself with a blunt knife than a sharp one. Also, for safety, keep them in a knife block or on a wall rack, rather than in among other utensils in a drawer.

11 If there are small children in the house keep all poisonous liquids, such as bleaches and household cleaners, in cupboards/cabinets fitted with childproof catches.

12 Slippery floors in the kitchen are a prime cause of accidents. Many manufacturers make "non-slip" tiles nowadays, so lay these in preference to other types, and if you have a wooden floor, use a non-slip polish. If oil, grease or water are spilled, clean them up immediately.

Finally, keep an emergency medical kit permanently in the kitchen, and store it in a place where everyone knows where it is. Buy a fire blanket and store it in an easily accessible place (not in a drawer or adjacent to the hob/cooktop). Never pour water over a pan fire, or try to remove the pan from the hob/cooktop. Turn off the hob/cooktop and smother the flames with a fire blanket, a damp cloth or towel or a large pan lid. Leave the kitchen, close the door behind you and, unless you are absolutely sure you have put out the fire, call the fire brigade.

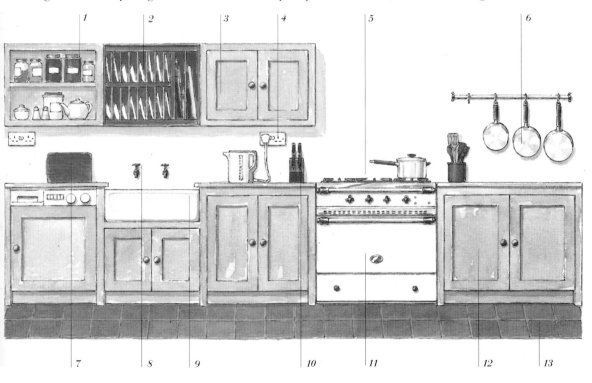

Planning Key Areas and Thinking Vertically

As discussed, when creating a period mood in your kitchen it is useful to have the *batterie de cuisine* and other kitchenalia on display. A certain amount of "clutter" adds to the mood but it is very easy to have too much. When planning the layout of a kitchen the aim should always be to store any utensil or ingredient that you use regularly as close as possible to the area or work zone that it is most often needed in. Moreover, whenever possible, it should be stored in a position that does not require you to overly bend, stretch or twist when reaching for it – in other words, in the space between just below hip height and just above shoulder height.

The diagram below illustrates two methods of storage in a small galley kitchen, and reveals how the use of storage space has been planned vertically, from the floor up. On the left is a traditional dresser, which is long and high, but not very deep, and therefore it does not project far into the room. Within the dresser the open space below the drawers has been utilized for larger storage bins and baskets. These could contain items such as fruit, vegetables and flour which al-though needed on a daily basis can be taken out or replenished without having to lift the containers themselves. Crockery and smaller and lighter storage containers sit on the open shelving and the work surface above the drawers, and are instantly accessible without any undue stretching or bending.

On the right, the use of vertical wall space has been maximized by combining standard base and wall cabinets with open shelving in between. Again, larger items, such as various pots and pans and casserole dishes, are stored on the lower shelves of the base cabinets, and lighter items on the higher shelves. Ideally, the base cabinet should be fitted with sliding, pull-out shelves, like the cutlery drawer), to minimize the amount of bending and stretching required to reach the contents. However, it has been fitted out with

500mm/20in

700mm/28in

900mm/36in

600mm/24in

Left: *In a narrow galley kitchen, a combination of traditional storage – in the form of a freestanding dresser – and floor- and wall-mounted cabinets, maximizes the amount of standing space in the centre. (Dressers are invariably tall and wide, but relatively shallow.) Also, the installation of open shelving between the wall and base cabinet maximizes the potential of storage space on the wall, keeps the most regularly used items close to hand, while leaving the front two-thirds of the work counter free for food preparation.*

Right: *The close proximity of generous cooking and food preparation zones promotes efficiency and safety.*

more than just one central shelf and makes the most of the space available.

Above the base cabinet, appliances in daily use, such as the toaster, are positioned at the back of the work surface – leaving the front two-thirds clear for preparing food and other tasks. The wall space above, and below the base of the wall cabinet, has been fully utilized by installing shelves to hold teacups, saucers and coffee cups – all of which are used frequently. In the wall cabinet above, drinking glasses sit above plates stored side-on in a plate-rack, rather than being stacked one on top of another, which would have required more effort to take them out and put them away.

Efficiency in the kitchen requires that you think vertically in each of the main work zones or work areas, particularly if space is restricted. The primary work zones are: a food preparation and washing up zone; a food mixing zone, and a cooking zone. The secondary zones are: a serving zone and, if there is space, an eating zone. Although all of these zones relate to each other, and in all but the largest of kitchens, often overlap, it is important to also consider them as self-sufficient areas. For example, in the kitchen shown below the mixing zone is intended for dry food preparation – largely related to baking – and the handling of food during cookery. Consequently, it features a sizeable work surface to accommodate mixing bowls and baking trays. The larger and heavier versions of these are stored in the cabinet below the work surface, while those utensils not placed in the jug at the back of the work surface are stored in the drawers. Various condiments, such as salt, pepper, and mustard, are within easy reach on the intermediate shelving, between the work surface and the wall cabinet, and the latter houses a variety of smaller jugs for liquids such as water, milk, sauces and gravy. Also, by siting the food preparation zone next to the cooking zone, heavy bowls and dishes do not need to be carried far as they are moved back and forth between the two.

On the following two pages there are further examples of how the various working zones are structured, and how they are positioned in relation to each other, for maximum ergonomic efficiency.

Above: *A freestanding dresser, converted to a washing-up zone by the incorporation of a sink inset into the base cabinet. The built-in plate rack above provides close-to-hand storage for regularly used china – and is an infinitely preferable alternative to stacking heavy plates on top of one another on a shelf in a cabinet.*

Above: *Even in large kitchens, where there is plenty of storage and work space, it is still important to think vertically. Here, glass-fronted, wall-mounted cabinets have been used to store regularly used crockery and china – the contents are visible and therefore easy to find and access.*

Right: *In this country kitchen, washing-up, food preparation and cooking zones are in a line – an arrangement recommended as one of the most ergonomically efficient by the Department of the Environment. The wall-hung storage rack places a wide range of kitchen utensils within easy reach of the cooker, the work counter and the sink.*

Left: *In many respects, glass-fronted cabinets provide one of the most efficient forms of storage for lighter items in daily or regular use in the kitchen. Glass-fronted cabinets combine the advantage of open shelving – the contents are visible – with that of cabinets with solid doors – the contents are protected from dust and dirt. For items such as salt, pepper, sugar etc, that you need to have easily to hand while preparing a meal or a drink, open shelves provide a slightly more practical alternative.*

Above: *The washing-up and food preparation corner of a U-shaped kitchen. Traditionally, sinks have wherever possible been installed under windows – natural light being safer and more pleasurable to work in.*

Above: *Again, washing-up, food preparation and cooking zones installed in a line, with wall-mounted ladder-racks and peg rails providing utensil storage in the optimum space between hip and shoulder height.*

Lighting

Prior to the 20th century lighting in kitchens was, when compared to what is available nowadays, inadequate (see Introduction, pages 8–17). From the Middle Ages right through to the end of the 19th century, candles, rush lights, tallow dips, oil lamps and the glow from the hearth were the chief sources of illumination. Even the installation of gas lighting in many urban houses towards the end of the 19th century left much to be desired, particularly in terms of air quality, safety and reliability of supply. It was only following the installation of a reliable supply of electricity into most households by the end of the second decade of the 20th century that the gloom of the average kitchen began to be dispelled.

On the grounds of safety and ease of working, it would be a mistake to spurn modern technology in favour of strict period authenticity. However, an acceptable compromise is to combine specific task lighting with general or background lighting. For task lighting use either fluorescent tubes or spotlights, preferably concealed under wall-mounted cupboards/cabinets or in the ceiling so as to illuminate surfaces designated for cooking and the preparation of food. General lighting can consist of original fittings (converted for electricity or rewired) or reproduction period light fittings (available in a wide range of period styles from specialist suppliers). Candles can also be used as background lighting and create an intimate atmosphere during evening meals.

Above: *An oil lamp suspended over the centre of the dining table provides illumination for both eating and preparing food.*

Above: *A cast-iron chandelier and a wrought iron and copper candelabrum provide period lighting during dinner.*

Right: *A traditional kitchen lightshade in many country areas: a prettily patterned glass cloth or tea towel.*

Above: *Wall lamps provide soft background lighting in one corner of this post-Modern kitchen.*

Left: *A combination of modern task lighting, provided by low-voltage spots on a ceiling track, and period pendant lights suspended over the table, provide ample illumination in this high-ceilinged kitchen.*

Below: *Recessed spot lights provide unobtrusive general and task lighting.*

Above: *Low-voltage spots or fluorescent tubes sited at intervals beneath wall-hung* cabinets illuminate the work surface for tasks such as washing up.

Woodgraining: Mahogany

Hardwoods such as mahogany and walnut with their intricate and decorative graining have always been in demand for furniture. However, because they are slow-growing demand has often outstripped supply. As their scarcity increased, which in some cases began as early as the 17th century, so they became increasingly expensive – especially mahogany and rosewood imported to Europe from South America, Cuba and the Far East.

One of the solutions to this problem was to simulate the graining and figuring of decorative hardwoods, using paints and glazes, on faster-growing and less expensive softwoods, such as pine and, nowadays, MDF. In Europe the demand for woodgraining began during the early part of the 17th century, and has remained a fashionable decorative technique ever since.

In its simplest form, woodgraining is little more than a pastiche of wood. However, when executed sympathetically, it can become a replication of the natural material that "tricks the eye" even under fairly close scrutiny. The example of mahogany graining shown here falls in to the latter category, in part because the technique employs water-based rather than oil-based glazes. Water-based glazes tend to produce a crisper, more authentic looking finish than the latter. However, they dry much faster, which means you have to complete each stage quite quickly. Consequently, you should thoroughly familiarise yourself with the mahogany grain, and practise the technique on spare off-cuts of wood, before beginning in earnest. For a detailed explanation of how to mix glazes, see page 118.

MATERIALS & EQUIPMENT
- Oil-based wood primer
- Oil-based undercoat
- Paints and glazes as listed below
- Clear gloss polyurethane varnish
- Clear satin polyurethane varnish
- 5cm/2in decorator's brush
- Small spalter (mottler) brush
- Badger softener brush
- 2.5cm/1in artist's brush
- Long-handled flogger brush
- 5cm/2in varnishing brush
- Ground chalk (whiting)
- Clean lint-free rag

A

B

C

D

PAINTS AND GLAZES
A Rusty-brown eggshell paint
B *Powder pigments:* 2 parts Van Dyke brown, 1 part raw umber, 1 part burnt umber. *Medium:* water. Ratios in glaze: 1 part pigment, 1 part medium.
C *Powder pigments:* 2 parts burnt umber, 1 part Van Dyke brown, 1 part raw umber. *Medium:* water. Ratios in glaze: 1 part pigment, 1 part medium.
D *Powder pigments:* 1 part Van Dyke brown, 1 part black. *Medium:* water. Ratios in glaze: 1 part pigment, 3 parts medium.

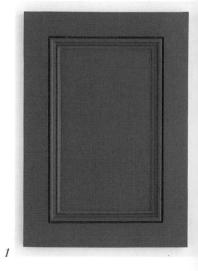

1

1 First make sure that you have an unblemished surface then prime and undercoat the door. Using a small decorator's brush, apply two coats of rusty-brown eggshell paint **A**, allowing each coat to dry for about 24 hours.

3

4

2 Wipe a thin coat of ground chalk (whiting) over the surface with a clean damp cloth.

3 Using a standard decorator's brush, roughly brush out glaze B over the middle panel and mouldings. Then drag a small spalter (mottler) through the glaze on the panel in a series of slightly overlapping vertical sweeps.

4 To create mahogany heart grain on the panel drag the spalter through the wet glaze in a series of overlapping elongated arcs. Start at the bottom of the panel and work upwards. Complete each arc in a continuous sweep, without pausing at the apex of a curve. Introduce subtle streaks of darker graining by occasionally dipping the bristles of the spalter into glaze C. (The heart grain will look more authentic if you slightly offset it to one side of the panel.)

5 Soften and blend the graining with a badger softener brush. Start at the bottom middle of the heart grain and lightly brush over the glaze in a series of short upward and outward sweeps (to the left and right), working your way up to the top of the panel. Keep removing build-up of glaze on the bristles with a damp rag.

5

6

7

8

6 Using an artist's brush, apply a little more of glazes B and C to the mouldings around the panel. Then, working on one section at a time – horizontals first, verticals second – drag the brush through the glaze in a continuous sweep from one mitred corner to the other.

7 Brush glaze B on to the top and bottom rails of the door frame. Then drag the mottler square-on through the glaze in a continuous horizontal sweep. (Darker streaks can be introduced by dipping into glaze C.) Immediately soften and blend the grain in the same direction with the badger softener, and keep cleaning the bristles with damp rag.

8 Repeat step 7 on the side rails of the frame, but this time drag the mottler at an angle through the glaze to accentuate the bands of graining.

9 Leave the glaze to dry for about 4 hours, then apply one coat of clear gloss polyurethane varnish with a varnishing brush and allow to dry for 24 hours.

10 Apply another coat of ground chalk (whiting). Brush glaze D on to the middle panel and moulding with a decorator's brush. Then drag the spalter vertically through the glaze as in step 3.

11 To create the small pores characteristic of mahogany graining, remove small flecks of glaze by lightly gripping a long-handled flogger parallel to the surface and, employing a loose wristy action, tap the bristles up and down the panel and moulding. (Keep cleaning the bristles on a damp rag.) Then repeat steps 10 and 11 on the rails of the frame – first the horizontals, and second the

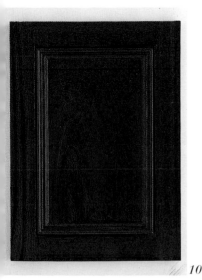

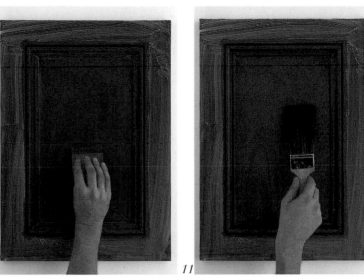

10

11

verticals – tapping gently in the direction of the grain.

12 The flogger removes small flecks of glaze to create the small pores characteristic of mahogany grain.

13 Leave to dry for about 4 hours, then apply one coat of either satin or gloss clear polyurethane varnish.

13

Woodgraining: Oak

MATERIALS & EQUIPMENT
- Oil-based wood primer
- Oil-based undercoat
- Paints and glazes as below
- White spirit (Mineral spirits)
- Transparent oil glaze
- Matte or satin clear polyurethane varnish
- 5cm (2in) standard decorator's brush
- Small badger softener brush
- 1cm (½in) flat fitch brush
- Varnishing brush
- Lint-free cotton rag

Like the mahogany graining demonstrated on pages 98–101, oak graining is a traditional method of simulating the attractive figuring and grain of the natural hardwood, using paints and glazes, on a cheaper and less decoratively interesting surface, such as a close-grained softwood or a man-made composite like MDF (medium density fibreboard).

In the example shown here a kitchen cupboard/cabinet door has been decorated to simulate oak graining. The middle panel of the door simulates the heart grain of oak. Like most other hardwoods the appearance of the figuring and grain varies, depending on which part of the tree it has come from and the way in which it has been cut – cutting wood horizontally or vertically produces quite distinct and different markings. Consequently, it is well worth your while studying as many examples of different cuts as possible – the technique shown for heart grain can then be adapted to simulate them.

When executed by a highly proficient decorative painter, woodgraining can deceive the onlooker, even when it is subjected to close scrutiny, into believing he or she is looking at the real thing. Probably the greatest exponent of the art was Thomas Kershaw who, at the Paris Exhibition of 1855, produced woodgrained furniture that was so realistic various French painters and members of the public thought he had actually used hardwood veneers rather than paint. (Some of the finest examples of his work can be seen at the Victoria & Albert museum in London). While you can not expect to match Kershaw's proficiency, by carefully following the illustrations here, and practising first on off-cuts of wood, it is possible to produce an authentic looking finish that, at the very least, will be substantially cheaper than buying real oak doors or furniture. For a detailed explanation of mixing paints and glazes, see page 118.

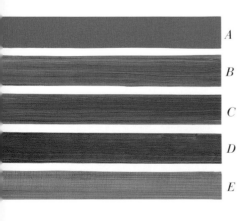

A
B
C
D
E

PAINTS AND GLAZES
A Bamboo coloured eggshell paint
B *Artist's oils:* 7 parts raw sienna, 3 parts raw umber.
Medium: 3 parts transparent oil glaze, 2 parts mineral spirits (white spirit). Ratios in glaze: 1 part pigments, 12 parts medium.
C *Artist's oils:* 2 parts raw sienna, 1 parts raw umber.
Medium: 4 parts transparent oil glaze, 5 parts mineral spirits. Ratios in glaze: 1 part pigment, 8 parts medium.
D *Artist's oils:* 2 parts raw sienna, 1 part raw umber.
Medium: 3 parts transparent oil glaze, 2 parts mineral spirits. Ratios in glaze: 1 part pigment, 7 parts medium.
E *Artist's oils:* 3 parts burnt umber, 1 part black.
Medium: 3 parts transparent oil glaze, 2 parts mineral spirits. Ratios in glaze: 1 part pigment, 40 parts medium.

2

1 Prime and undercoat the door and leave to dry.
Brush on two coats of paint A with a standard
decorator's brush, allowing up to 24 hours drying time
after each coat. Next, using a standard decorator's
brush, roughly brush out pale brown glaze B over the
middle panel and top and bottom rails of the door.

2 Drag the bristles of a standard decorator's brush
through the glaze in a series of slightly
overlapping parallel sweeps to establish the direction
of the grain. Complete the middle panel first –
vertically; then the top and bottom rails of the frame –
horizontally; and finally, the side rails – vertically. At
the end of each sweep of the brush wipe the bristles on
a lint-free cotton rag dampened with mineral spirits
(white spirit) to remove the build-up of glaze.

3 To grain the middle panel lightly grip a badger
softener brush and, using a loose wristy action, tap
(flog) the sides of the bristles up and down the surface
in a series of slightly overlapping, vertical parallel
bands. As in step 3, keep cleaning the bristles on a rag
dampened with mineral spirits to remove the build up
of glaze. Next, repeat the technique on the top and
bottom rails of the door, and then on the side rails –
always in the direction of the grain. Leave the surface
to dry for approximately 24 hours.

3

4

5

Note: the flogging action in step 3 (on the previous page) removes flecks of wet glaze from the surface to create the small, irregular-shaped pores characteristic of oak grain.

4 Wipe a thin coat of transparent oil glaze over the panel of the door with a lint-free cotton rag. Allow it to become tacky (this should take about 15 minutes) and then start to paint the oak heart grain using glaze C and a flat fitch brush. Begin just off-centre and work outwards, using the illustration for guidance as to the composition. (Again, it is best to practise this technique first on a spare off-cut of wood.)

5 Having completed about one third of the panel, lightly flick the bristles of a small badger softener over the wet glaze. Work from in to out – in other words,

always towards the enclosed heart of the grain.

6 Repeat steps 4 and 5 until you have completed the graining on the panel. Then lightly flog the entire surface with a small badger softener to remove flecks of glaze from the surface, using the technique described in step 3.

7 Apply glaze D to the four rails of the door with a standard decorator's brush. Next, drag the brush a slight angle through the glaze to accentuate the darker and lighter bands of graining. As before, complete the top and bottom rails first, followed by the sides – always dragging in the direction of the grain and removing excess glaze from the bristles on a rag dampened in mineral spirits at the end of each drag. Then lightly flog the rails with a badger softener as in step 3.

8 Leave the surface to dry for approximately 24 hours. Then apply one coat of either matte or satin clear polyurethane varnish, using a varnishing brush.

9 Alternatively, if you wish to artificially age the surface, brush on a coat of antiquing glaze E, building up a thicker layer in the recesses around the middle panel, before applying the varnish referred to in step 8.

7

9

Period Finishes: Colourwashing

Paint finishes, some of which date back to the 17th and 18th centuries, are enjoying a renaissance Colourwashing is a traditional paint finish used to decorate walls and, as here, wooden furniture. The technique involves making up a glaze or diluting a paint to create a semi-translucent veil of colour that allows underlying colours and patterns – in this case the figuring and grain of natural wood – to ghost through it. Historically the finish is associated with country furniture, particularly those found in the rural areas of Scandinavia, Europe and North America. However, it has also been used in urban kitchens and on built-in cupboards/cabinets.

Traditionally, distemper was employed for colourwashing. However, its poor durability,

---

MATERIALS & EQUIPMENT
- Dark mahogany water-based wood stain
- Clear matte or satin acrylic varnish
- 5cm/2in decorator's brush
- 5cm/2in varnishing brush
- Lint-free cotton rag

A

PAINT
A Dark green, matte finish buttermilk paint, diluted 1:1 with water.

1

2

1 If you do not wish to apply an antiquing glaze omit this stage and go straight to step 2.

To artificially age the pine door, dilute a dark mahogany coloured, water-based wood stain with

particularly in humid or damp conditions, and an unfortunate tendency when applied to furniture to rub off on contact with clothing, led painters and decorators to search for more effective alternatives. One of these was buttermilk paint, notably favoured by itinerant craftsmen on the eastern seaboard of North America during the 18th and 19th centuries. Today, a number of specialist paint manufacturers are reproducing buttermilk paints in authentic period colours (for names and addresses, see the Directory, pages 122–5), and one of these has been used for the project illustrated here. You should also note that for this project the pine door was first artificially aged (darkened) by the application of an antiquing glaze – this is an optional step. However, it does produce a more subtle and mellow finish than if you were to apply the colourwash directly on to untreated new pine. As this is a matter of personal choice, you are advised to try out the technique on an off-cut of pine before decorating a cabinet door or any other item of furniture in your kitchen.

water, 1:1. Using a small decorator's brush in one hand, apply the stain over the surface of the door. Almost immediately, follow up the brushwork by rubbing the stain into the surface with a pad of lint-free cotton rag held in the other hand. Rub broadly in the direction of the grain, and work as quickly as you can because the stain will become touch-dry quite quickly.

In addition to rubbing in the stain, at this stage you are also removing any excess to create a semi-translucent finish that allows the underlying grain of the wood to ghost through. So, keep turning or replacing the cotton pad as it becomes clogged with the diluted stain. Then leave the surface to dry thoroughly for approximately four hours, depending on humidity and room temperature.

2 For the colourwash, using a small decorator's brush, apply paint A and (as in step 1) almost immediately follow up th brushwork by rubbing it into the surface, in the direction of the grain, with a pad of lint-free cotton rag. As before you are as much removing paint as rubbing it in, to allow the underlying colour and grain of the wood to ghost through – so keep turning and changing the cotton pad as it becomes clogged.

3

3 Leave the surface to dry thoroughly for about 12 hours. To finish the door brush on a coat of clear matte or satin acrylic varnish to protect against moisture, humidity and general

Period Finishes: Dragging

Dragging is a traditional paint finish primarily used on joinery and items of furniture. The technique involves pulling or dragging the bristles of a brush through a wet glaze in a series of roughly parallel sweeps to create a striped finish that is not only aesthetically pleasing, but is also used as a simulation of woodgrain.

Unlike the mahogany and oak wood graining demonstrated on pages 98–102, where the intention is to produce a pretty accurate simulation or replication of the figuring and graining of natural wood, dragging has always been seen as something of a pastiche. Viewed across a room some examples might appear at first glance to look like woodgrain, but the trompe l'oeil effect – or "trick of the eye" – rapidly breaks down on closer inspection. However, this is the intention – the fairly obvious deception being viewed, certainly by decorative painters, as an amusing theatrical effect. Indeed, a substantial amount of the dragged joinery and furniture found in rural European, Scandinavian and North American homes during the late 17th, 18th and 19th centuries was executed in a range of colours that bore little or no relation to the colouring of natural wood.

In the example shown here, a kitchen cupboard/cabinet door made of MDF (medium density fibreboard) has been dragged in tones of pastel grey-blue – colours often associated with rustic Scandinavian interiors. The dragging is also very faint, or subtle. If you wish to produce a bolder finish with more obvious lines of grain, you should press more firmly as you drag the brush through the wet glaze, and restrict yourself to a single, continuous drag on each section, rather than lightly working the brush back and forth. For a detailed explanation of how to mix glazes, refer to page 112.

A

B

C

PAINTS AND GLAZES
A *Artist's oils:* 1 part raw umber, 2 parts black, 5 parts cobalt blue. *Medium:* 1 part transparent oil glaze, 1 part white spirit. Ratio: 1 part artist's oils to 11 parts medium.
B As glaze A, but lightened by mixing 1:1 with white eggshell.
C *Artist's oils:* 1 part Van Dyke brown, 1 part black. *Medium:* 4 parts transparent oil glaze. Ratio: 1 part artist's oils to 4 parts medium.

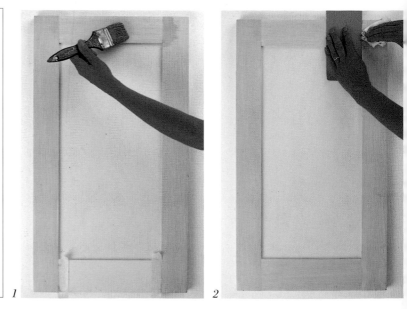

1

2

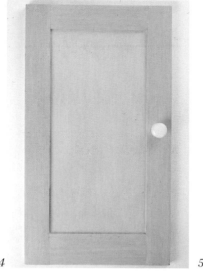

4

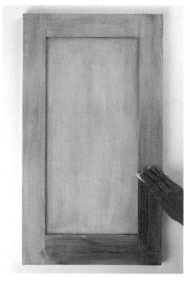

5

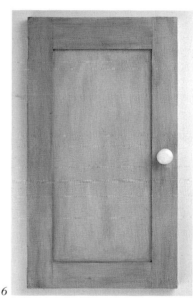

6

1 Having primed and undercoated the door and allowed the surface to dry thoroughly, apply one or two coats of pale blue-gray eggshell paint. Allow up to 24 hours drying time after each coat. Next, using a small decorator's brush, apply glaze A to the top, bottom and side rails of the door. Work on one rail at a time, and lightly drag the bristles of the brush back and forth through the glaze – vertically for the side rails and horizontally for the top and bottom rails.

Because you are trying to mimic the appearance of wood grain you will be removing faint streaks of glaze with the brush. To achieve this, keep the bristles as dry as possible as you drag the brush back and forth, by regularly removing excess glaze from the bristles on a piece of lint-free cotton rag.

2 To create the butt joints where the rails meet at the four corners of the door frame, carefully position a piece of coarse sandpaper face down on top of the still-wet glaze and along the line of the joint. Fold a piece of lint-free cotton rag to create a thin, straight edge and,

holding the sandpaper lightly but firmly in place, gently drag the edge of the rag along the edge of the paper. This will remove a minute amount of glaze and create a faint straight line dividing two adjoining rails. Next, carefully lift off the sandpaper without disturbing the underlying glaze, and repeat on the other three corners, using new paper and rag for each one. Then leave to dry for approximately 24 hours.

3 Using the lighter blue glaze B and a small decorator's brush, lightly drag the middle panel of the door. As in step 1 work the bristle tips vertically up and down the panel, regularly removing the build up of glaze on the brush with a lint-free cotton rag. Again, allow to dry for approximately 24 hours.

4 If you are happy with the appearance of the door, apply a coat of clear matte or satin acrylic varnish to protect against moisture, humidity and general wear and tear.

5 Alternatively, you can artificially age the door by brushing on a coat of antiquing glaze C and wiping off the excess

with a pad of lint-free cotton rag. The aim of the antiquing glaze being to create a thin, translucent veil of colour that darkens the finish while allowing the underlying glazes to ghost through it. Leave to dry for between 12–24 hours, depending on room temperature.

6 If you have missed out step 4 in order to apply the antiquing glaze in step 5, finish the door by applying a coat of clear matte or satin acrylic varnish for protection.

Period Finishes: Stencilling

Stencilling, a technique for transferring a motif or pattern onto a contrasting coloured background by applying paint through a cut-out stencil card, dates back to *c.* 3000 BC. In Europe, stencilling has been used as a form of decoration from medieval times to the present day and has been applied to a wide variety of surfaces.

The Art Nouveau pre-cut stencil used in this project to decorate a kitchen cupboard door was inspired by a Charles Rennie Mackintosh design from around the turn of the century. Together with many other period stencils, it was produced by a modern specialist stencil company (see the Directory pages 122-5), and is entitled Glasgow Roses. The simplicity and fluidity of the design together with the traditional colours used – pink, green and black – make this stencil particularly suited to a kitchen in a late-19th or early 20th-century house or villa.

MATERIALS & EQUIPMENT
- Pre-cut stencil
- Small pieces of sponge
- Oil-based eggshell paint
- Acrylic stencil paints
- Masking (drafting) tape
- Two 1.25cm/½in brushes
- Three old saucers
- Clean lint-free rag
- Piece of lining paper
- Matte, clear acrylic varnish & varnish brush

A

B

C

D

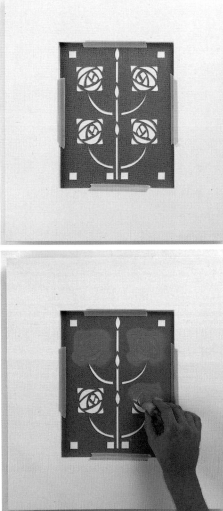

1

2

ACRYLIC STENCIL PAINTS
A **Mid-pink**
B **As A** above, plus a little black to darken
C **Mid-green**, plus a little black to darken
D **Black**

The paints used were specifically designed for stencilling and are relatively quick-drying. (See pages 120–5 for suppliers.) Use the colour swatches above for reference, but ultimately adjust to suit your own requirements.

1 Having prepared the door, apply two coats of oil-based white eggshell paint and allow to dry thoroughly after each coat. Then secure the edges of the stencil card in position with masking (drafting) tape. (To minimize the risk of the tape lifting any of the paint when it is removed, make it less tacky by pressing it down on a clean rag before applying.)

2 Pour a little pink paint (A) into a saucer, dab a piece of sponge into it and remove any excess on a spare piece of lining paper. (Do not saturate the sponge, or paint will creep under the edges of the stencil.) Lightly sponge over the roses, one by one. To introduce subtle shading to the edges of the roses, mix a darker pink (B) and apply as before.

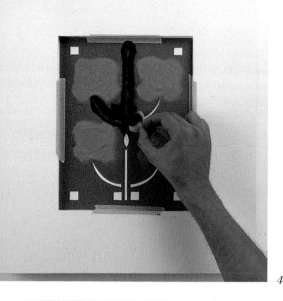

4

3 Mix the green-black paint (C) in a saucer and, when you are happy with the colour, apply to the central stalk and stems, using the same technique and a new piece of sponge.

4 Again, using a fresh piece of sponge, apply black paint (D) to the squares either side of the base of the stalk and at the four corners of the stencil.

5 Once the paint has dried thoroughly (this may take up to one hour), carefully remove the masking (drafting) tape and peel back the stencil card. Although stencil paints are relatively hard-wearing, because of the need to regularly wipe down surfaces in kitchens, apply a coat of clear matte or mid-sheen acrylic varnish to the entire door.

Period Finishes: Fake Limewash

As a protective and decorative finish for plaster, render, masonry, and to a lesser extent wood, limewash has been in common use for thousands of years, the earliest examples having been found on primitive dwellings c. 8000 BC.

First and foremost, limewash has an aesthetically pleasing appearance which, depending on the light, the weather and the pigments used, can range from a dazzling luminous white, best associated with the vernacular architecture of the Mediterranean, to a darker, matte, chalky colour when wet or under overcast conditions, such as often prevail in Northern Europe. Second, the addition of a wide range of pigments – primarily earth colours and by-products of the mining industry, such as iron-oxide, cobalt and copper carbonate – which are enhanced by the limewash base, produces a superb vitality and purity of colour, and a pleasant mellowing with age. Thirdly, limewash allows the underlying surface to breathe, which is vital for the survival of traditional cob walls – if trapped, moisture will soon rot them.

However, during its preparation and, to some extent its application, limewash is toxic. Moreover, the relatively high levels of humidity and moisture often found in kitchens means it is not particularly durable. A more practical alternative, using modern synthetic paints and a distressing technique, is the simulated limewash finish demonstrated here. It has none of the drawbacks of traditional limewash, while conveying an authentic appearance. (Although for the reasons stated above, it must not be used on any surface, such as the cob walls of a country cottage, that need to breathe in order to survive.)

1 **Prepare the walls by washing with sugar soap. Using a large decorator's brush, apply one or two coats of paint A. Allow each coat to dry for approximately 4 hours. Dip the bristle tips of a large decorator's brush into paint B and, having brushed off most of the paint on a piece of lining paper, dry-brush what is**

A

B

C

PAINTS AND GLAZES
A Off-white or very pale yellow latex (matte emulsion) paint.
B 3 parts light brown eggshell paint, 1 part mineral spirits (white spirit).
C Pale beige latex (matte emulsion) paint.

1

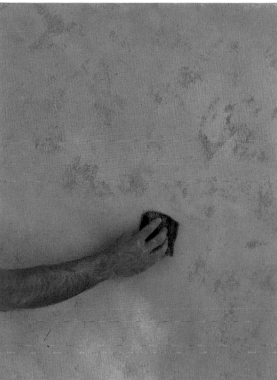

3

left in all directions over the walls. Repeat this procedure until you have built up a mottled, cloudy expanse of colour. Leave to dry for 12–16 hours.

2 Repeat the technique used in step 1, using pale beige paint C. However, this time leave more paint on the bristles in order to produce a smoother, less brushy looking coat which allows very little of the underlying colour to show through. Then leave to dry.

3 Dampen a plastic kitchen scourer with water and scrub down the wall. This will soften up the top coat, cutting it back in places to reveal patches of the underlying colour, as well as spreading a thin, translucent veil of the top colour over the entire surface. When finished, allow to dry for about 8 hours.

4 To protect the walls from moisture, and general wear and tear, apply a coat of clear matte acrylic varnish.

4

Period Finishes: Ragging

MATERIALS AND EQUIPMENT
- Oil-based white or pale pink undercoat
- Clear matte or satin acrylic varnish
- 10cm/4in decorator's brush
- Large badger softener brush
- Large varnishing brush
- Lint-free cotton rag
- Paints and glazes as below

Over the past decade or so, ragging has become one of the most popular of the "broken colour" finishes, and has been used in both rural and urban settings The technique, in the example shown here, involves distressing an oil-based glaze with a lint-free cotton rag moistened with solvent. The result is a subtle, random pattern or imprint in the glaze which, being semi-translucent, allows a different coloured opaque basecoat to ghost through it. Variations in pattern and texture can be produced by using the same technique and rags made from materials as diverse as hessian, muslin, silk and even polythene or plastic.

From an historical point of view, ragging is essentially a simulation of what happens over a period of time to many of the chemically unstable traditional paints used prior to the 20th century – prolonged exposure to changes in light and humidity resulting in a chemical breakdown of pigments that gives a painted surface an aesthetically pleasing mottled appearance.

You should note that because of the fairly rapid drying time of the glaze used, when ragging a large surface area, such as the walls of a kitchen, it is best carried out by two people: one person to brush on and soften the glaze; another to follow behind distressing with the rag. For a detailed explanation of how to mix a glaze, see page 118.

A

B

PAINTS AND GLAZES
For the method of mixing glazes see page 118.

A Terracotta coloured, oil-based eggshell paint.
B *Artists oils:* 6 parts burnt sienna, 1 part alizarin crimson. *Medium:* 3 parts transparent oil glaze, 2 parts white spirit (mineral spirits). Ratios in glaze: 1 part artists oils, 8 parts medium.

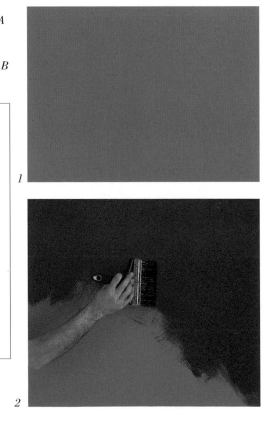

1

2

1 **To carry out a decorative finish you need an unblemished surface. Prepare the wall by stripping off any wallpaper and filling any holes or cracks with filler (speckle). Once the wall is smooth prime it with a thin wash of emulsion paint. Allow to dry thoroughly. You can now apply two coats of terracotta coloured paint A, using a large decorator's brush. Leave the wall to dry for about 24 hours after each coat.**

2 **Again using a large standard decorator's brush, apply one coat of red glaze B over the wall. Do not worry about leaving any brush marks in the glaze.**

4

3 Working as quickly as you can, lightly brush a large badger softener brush in all directions over the wet surface in order to soften and blend the glaze and disguise any brush marks.

4 Make up a crumpled pad of lint-free cotton rag and lightly dab it over the wet surface to remove irregular-shaped patches of glaze. Keep reforming or replacing the pad when it becomes clogged with glaze. Depending on the room temperature you have about half-an-hour to distress the glaze with the rag before it starts to become unworkable, so work as quickly as you can.

5 Finally leave the surface to dry for roughly 24 hours, and then apply one or two coats of clear matte or satin acrylic varnish to protect against moisture and general wear and tear. Allow a minimum of 4 hours drying time between coats.

5

Decorating a Plate Rack

Plate racks are featured in many of the period-style kitchens in this book. Freestanding or wall-mounted plate racks can be bought from specialist kitchen suppliers and many leading department stores. They are usually made of pale coloured soft and hardwoods such as pine or beech, and are sometimes finished with clear varnish to provide protection against moisture.

If you have painted cupboards/cabinets in the kitchen it is quite a simple task to decorate a plate rack in a matching or harmonious colour. The technique illustrated here involves diluting an oil-based paint with white spirit (mineral spirits) so that it becomes semi-translucent. When applied to the plate rack it thus allows the underlying colour of the wood to ghost through – in effect a colourwash rather than a flat coat of opaque paint. Obviously any colour can be used. However, you should use an oil- rather than a water-based paint, as the latter may raise the grain (or roughen) the surface of the wood.

A

PAINT
A Mid-blue oil-based eggshell paint, diluted in a ratio of 3:2 with white spirit (mineral spirits)

1

1 **Ideally the plate rack should be made of an unfinished light-coloured wood, such as pine or beech. The darker the wood the more it will change the colour of the applied paint. Also, if the wood has been waxed you will need to remove this by rubbing down a rag dampened with** **mineral spirits (white spirit) – otherwise paint will fail to properly adhere to the surface. Similarly, wood that has been varnished must first be rubbed down with a medium or coarse grade silicon carbide (wet-and-dry) paper to key the surface for the paint.**

3

2 Using a small decorator's brush, apply diluted blue paint A. Work on only a few bars or a small section at a time.

3 While the paint is still wet on the first few bars or small section, and before it become tacky, rub it into the wood and wipe off any excess with a pad of lint-free cotton rag. You are trying to create a thin, semi-translucent veil of colour that allows the underlying wood to ghost through it, so keep turning and replacing the pad as it becomes clogged with paint. Repeat in stages for the rest of the rack, and then allow to dry thoroughly for approximately 24 hours.

4 Finally, apply one or two coats of clear matte or satin finish polyurethane varnish to protect the paint from moisture and general wear and tear. Allow 24 hours drying time after each coat.

4

Mixing Paints and Glazes

To produce many of the decorative paint finishes shown in Kitchen Practicalities, you will need to mix various oil- and water-based glazes. The glazes are made up of pigments suspended in a clear medium and sufficiently thinned with a solvent to make them semi-transparent when applied over an opaque basecoat. The tinted semi-transparent glaze allows the underlying ground colour to "ghost" through it, thereby creating subtle combinations, depths and gradations of colour.

The recipe for each glaze gives the approximate proportions of each pigment in relation to any other pigments included, the approximate proportions of solvent in relation to the clear medium, and the approximate proportions of combined pigments in relation to the combined solvent and medium. For example, in glaze B used to produce the oak graining finish shown on pages 102–5 the pigment consists of 7 parts raw sienna artist's oil to 3 parts raw umber artist's oil. The medium consists of 3 parts transparent oil glaze to 2 parts white spirit (mineral spirits). When mixed together the proportion (or ratio) of combined pigments to medium in the glaze equals 1 part pigments to 12 parts medium.

The actual quantity of glaze you require depends upon the size and absorbency of the underlying surface, and how thickly you apply the glaze. Consequently, it is virtually impossible to prescribe exact quantities. However, a useful rule of thumb is: 250ml (½ pint) of glaze to cover a surface of approximately 7 sq m (7½ sq ft).

MIXING AN OIL-BASED GLAZE:

To mix approximately 250ml (½ pint) of glaze B for oak graining you should:

1 Using a old artist's fitch brush to blend them thoroughly, mix 150ml of transparent oil glaze with 100ml of white spirit (mineral spirits) to make the medium. In other words, mix them in a ratio of 3:2. Do this in a 1 litre (½ gallon) metal or plastic paint kettle.

2 Squeeze the artist's oils from their tubes into another container. The pigments (artist's oils) are mixed together in a ratio of 7 parts raw sienna to 3 parts raw umber.

3 Pour a little of the blended clear medium into a third container and, again using an old artist's fitch, slowly blend in the pigments (artist's oils) from the second container. You will end up with a coloured liquid of cream-like consistency that should match the relevant colour swatch shown against the recipe for the glaze (see page 102). At this stage do not worry about the translucency of the glaze – just the colour match. Add more pigments if required.

4 Again using an old artist's fitch, gradually stir the coloured, cream-like liquid in the third container into the bulk of the clear medium that remains in the first container. From time to time swatch a little of the colour over the bamboo-coloured eggshell basecoat to test the translucency of the glaze. Add more medium to increase the translucency and more pigment(s) to increase the opacity, but in each case make sure you thoroughly blend the mixture.

Note: The oil-based glaze described above contains artist's oils and transparent oil glaze, and is generally used by professional specialist decorators. However, you can also mix an oil-based glaze by using flat-oil or eggshell paint, either pre-mixed or tinted to the desired colour with artist's oils, and thinned to the required degree of translucency by the addition of white spirit (mineral spirit).

MIXING A WATER-BASED ANTIQUING GLAZE:

To mix the water-based glaze B used for mahogany graining on pages 98–101 you should:

1 Mix 2 parts Van Dyke brown artist's powder pigment to 1 part raw umber artist's powder pigment and 1 part burnt umber artist's powder pigment, adding a little water until you have a coloured liquid with the consistency of cream.

2 Pour water into a separate container – the volume required is the same as the volume of coloured liquid in the first container

3 Gradually add the medium in the second container to the coloured liquid in the first container to produce the glaze, blending thoroughly as you go. Keep testing the glaze for strength of colour on an off-cut of wood primed with the rusty-brown eggshell basecoat. Add a little more pigment if you wish to darken it.

Glossary

Aesthetic Movement: A decorative arts movement with a strong Japanese influence. Flourished in Britain from *c.*1870 to the late 1880s. A precursor of Art Nouveau, it also overlapped with the Arts and Crafts Movement.

American Colonial style: Style of architecture, decoration and furniture in the North American Colonies from the early 17th-century pioneer settlements to the establishment of a Federal Government in 1789.

American Federal style: Style of architecture, decoration and furniture prevalent from the early years of American independence (1789-1830); often incorporates patriotic and military symbols.

Antiquing: Technique for artificially ageing surfaces using paints and glazes.

Armoire: The French name for a large cabinet, cupboard or linen press.

Art Deco: Style of decorative art particularly associated with the 1920s and '30s, which developed the curvilinearity of Art Nouveau into more streamlined geometrical forms.

Art Nouveau: Style of decoration characterized by curves and flowing lines, asymmetry and flower and leaf motifs, prevalent from the 1880s to 1914.

Arts and Crafts Movement: Led by a group of artists and craftsmen, from approximately 1860 to 1925, who rejected machine-made, mass-produced items in favour of those made by traditional methods. Drew on pre-industrial periods and styles for inspiration.

Aumbry: Medieval word for a cupboard built into a recess or niche in a wall. The doors were often pierced for ventilation.

Baluster: A small pillar, usually circular in section and curvaceous in outline.

Ballcock: Inserted in a cistern or water tank, consists of a hollow metal or plastic ball that rises and falls with the flow of water, and shuts off the supply when the required level is reached.

Baronial-style: Also known as "monastic style". Popular during the late 19th century and refers to a heavy, mock-Gothic style of architecture, decoration and furniture that drew on ecclesiastical designs, particularly Medieval.

Batterie de cuisine: Collective term for pots, pans, spoons, ladles and other accessories used for the preparation of food.

Beaux Arts Movement: Flourished in the United States between 1876 and 1930, and encompassed a variety of historical architectural styles. Led by American architects, such as Richard Morris Hunt, who had studied at the Ecole des Beaux Arts in Paris. Styles included French and Italian Renaissance, and Elizabethan, Georgian, Regency, English Gothic and Spanish revival, allied with modern materials and methods of construction.

Betty lamp: American boat-shaped oil lamp.

Biedermeier: A style of furniture and interior decoration, glass and porcelain, that appeared in Austria and Germany after the Napoleonic wars. Furniture was mostly hand-crafted in walnut and softwoods such as cherry and pear, and displayed geometric forms and, often, sophisticated motifs.

Black leading: A black coloured mineral (plumbago) used to "polish" cast-iron grates and ranges.

Butt joint: A joint formed between the squared ends of two items which come together but do not overlap.

Buttery: Ancillary room off a kitchen, used to manufacture dairy products.

Caddy: An airtight box or jar for storing tea or coffee.

Capstan: A type of tap (faucet) handle, in the shape of a cross.

Chippendale-style: Furniture and architectural fixtures and fittings made to the designs of Thomas Chippendale (1718–89). They display a variety of influences, including Chinese, Rococo and Gothic styles.

Cob: A mixture of clay and straw, once used for walls.

Colander: A perforated vessel, usually made of metal, and used for straining and draining the water from cooked vegetables.

Colourwashing: Technique for decorating wooden and plaster surfaces, using layers of semi-translucent paint and glazes, which allows the underlying colour or grain to ghost through.

Cornice: In Classical architecture, the projecting top of an entablature.

Crumb cloth: A cloth temporarily laid over a floor or carpet, usually under a dining table, and designed to catch spills and crumbs.

Damper: A shutter that can be opened or closed to regulate a draught.

Dado: Either a rail running around the walls of a room at approximately the height of a chair back, or the space on the wall below that rail and above the baseboard or skirting board.

Deal: Fir or pine.

Dentil: One of a series of small blocks (dentillations) used to form an ornamental row, and primarily used in Corinthian, Ionic and Composite mouldings.

Distemper: An early form of water-based paint, rather like modern emulsion (latex) paint.

Domo: Latin for house.

Drab: A light grayish-brown or greenish-brown coloured paint.

Dragging: Technique for crudely simulating the appearance of wood grain, and achieved by dragging a brush through a still-wet, semi-transparent paint or glaze to partly reveal a contrasting coloured base coat.

Drop-leaf table: Table that can be increased or reduced in size by raising or lowering hinged leaves.

Dumb waiter: A movable platform or trolley for transporting food either to or around a dining room.

Dutch oven: A heavy, lidded cooking pot, originally heated by partly submerging it in hot coals.

Ebonized: Wood stained and polished black to simulate ebony.

Edwardian: A style of architecture and decoration prevalent in England between 1901 and 1910.

Egg tempera: Early form of emulsion (latex) paint, made by mixing pigments with linseed oil, water and egg yolk. Primarily used on furniture.

Empire style: A style of architecture, furniture and decoration popular in France between 1804–30, and the United States between 1810–30, and characterized by the use of sombre, heavy-looking woods, such as mahogany, ebony and rosewood; mostly uncarved but generously ornamented with motifs such as burning torches, urns, lion masks, eagles and swans, papyrus leaves, crocodiles, sphinxes and other Egyptian motifs. In the United States the style was adapted to include local motifs such as fruit, flowers and the eagle.

Encaustic tiles: Earthenware tiles patterned with inlays of coloured clay slips.

Entablature: In Classical architecture the part above the columns, made up of an architrave, frieze and cornice.

Epoxy resin: A glue or adhesive containing synthetic polymers.

Etruscan-style: A late 18th-century offshoot of neo-Classicism introduced by Robert Adam *c*.1774, and based on the architecture, ornamental wares and style of decoration originating in Etruria (now Tuscany and Umbria), in Italy.

Faïence: Tin-glazed earthenware.

Faux marble: The art of simulating the appearance of marble on surfaces, using paints and glazes.

Festoon: See **Swag.**

Fillet: Small space or band used in or alongside a decorative moulding of wood, plaster, metal or stone.

Fire dogs: Pair of metal supports for logs in a fireplace; also called andirons.

Fire irons: Fireplace tools, such as a shovel, poker and tongs, etc.

Firehood: A canopy installed over a hearth or cooking range, designed to channel smoke and fumes up a flue and away from the room.

Flat iron: An old-fashioned iron for pressing clothes, heated on the stove.

Flemish bond: Brickwork in which headers (short face visible) and stretchers (long face visible) alternate on each course of bricks.

Floorcloth: Canvas sheeting painted to look like a more expensive floor covering, such as marble, tiles, wood or carpet.

Flue: A cavity in a chimneybreast, or a pipe, used to convey smoke, hot gases and flames from a fire to outside of a building.

Frieze: The middle section of an entablature, or the area on a wall below cornice and above picture rail.

Fruitwood: The wood of a fruit tree, such as apple, cherry or pear.

Gate-leg table: Table with a hinged and framed leg that can be swung in or out to raise up or let down a table leaf.

Georgian style: An 18th-century style characterized by the use of proportions and ornaments of Classical architecture.

Gilding: A wafer-thin covering of gold leaf, or a gold-like substance.

Gothic-revival: A 19th-century revival of Gothic forms, led by Augustus Pugin, William Burges, William Morris, and Charles Eastlake. Gothic architecture and decoration originally flourished from the 11th to the 15th century and was characterized by soaring, slender lines, pointed or ogee arches and tracery.

Hastener: A semi-circular metal reflector attached to early cast-iron ranges and designed to reflect heat onto a joint roasting on a spit.

Herlebecheria: The Latin word for scullery; it was commonly used during the Middle Ages.

Herringbone: Style of brickwork or masonry laid so the bricks or stones slope in different directions in alternate rows – looks like the spine of a herring.

Inglenook: Recessed space beside a fireplace, usually housing one or two wooden or stone benches.

Jacobean: A style of architecture and decoration characteristic of the reign of James I (1603–25).

Latticework: A network of crossed laths or bars used as ornamentation.

Limewash: A traditional paint made of slaked lime, water and pigment, and used to coat porous plaster and stone walls.

Linoleum: A durable floor covering made from compressed cork, ground wood and linseed oil, fixed to a burlap or strong canvas backing. Often decorated to simulate more expensive material, such as marble.

Love spoon: A wooden spoon, traditionally carved by a young man and given as a gift to a loved one.

Medieval: Commonly used to refer to the period of history known as the Middle Ages: 476 AD, from the fall of the last Western Roman emperor, Constantine, to 1453, the start of the Italian Renaissance.

MDF: Medium density fibreboard, made from compressed particles of wood and used in the construction of furniture and architectural fixtures and fittings.

Milk paint: Also known as buttermilk or casein paint. Made by mixing earth-coloured pigments with buttermilk or skimmed milk, and a little lime. Popular in country areas of North America during the late 18th and 19th century, and commonly found in Colonial-style interiors.

Modernism: Self-conscious style created by architects of the Modern Movement, inspired by a need to break with the past and to express the spirit of the machine age. Rejected ornamentation in favour of space, proportion and smooth surfaces. Began *c.*1920 and had been partly rejected by *c.*1960.

Neo-Classical: A style of architecture and decoration based on the forms of ancient Greece and Rome. Characteristic motifs include garlands of flowers and husks, palmettes, anthemions, round and oval paterae, urns and cameos.

Palladian: An interpretation of the Classical style developed by the Italian architect Andrea Palladio (1508–80). Bought to England by Inigo Jones in the 17th century, revived in the early 18th century by Lord Burlington and Colen Campbell, and influenced American architecture in the late 18th century.

Pantry: A small room off a kitchen, used to store food and tablewares.

Parlour: A family sitting room or living room.

Pentize: Covered walkway.

Pier: Support for a lintel or an arch, or other fixtures and fittings, such as a sink.

Pilaster: Usually a flat rectangular classical column.

Post-Modernism: A reaction against Modernism (see above). Began in the 1950s, and promotes the reintroduction of bright colours and ornamental architec-tural components that are not necessarily functional. Draws on a wide range of styles from previous centuries, and adapts and combines them in innovative ways.

PVA: A water-based adhesive.

Quarry tile: A square unglazed floor tile.

Ragging: Technique for creating subtle random patterns on painted surfaces by dabbing a rag up and down in a wet translucent glaze applied over a contrasting coloured ground coat.

Raised and fielded panels: A panel, usually in the middle of a door, with a plain raised centre.

Range: An enclosed kitchen fireplace or cooker incorporating ovens, hot plates and, often, a roasting spit.

Refectory table: Long narrow dining table supported on two shaped pillars, one at each end.

Rush-lights: A candle or night light with a wick made of rush-pith.

Santa Fé style: A style of architecture, furniture and interior design which draws on designs and motifs found in early South American civilizations. Popular on the west coast of America, north and south of the border.

Sconce: A wall bracket used to hold candles and other forms of lighting.

Scullery: Ancillary room off a kitchen, primarily used for washing kitchen wares and clothing.

Settle: A long high-backed wooden bench.

Shaker style: Furniture and decoration inspired by the products of the Shaker communities in North America. High standards of craftsmanship are combined with designs that have no superfluous ornamentation.

Skillet: A small long-handled frying pan.

Sprigged cotton: Cotton, embroidered or printed with a spray of leaves or flowers.

Stencilling: The art of applying a pattern or motif to a surface by painting it on through holes in a piece of card, the holes making up the shape of the pattern or motif in question.

Stick-back chair: A chair with a back made up of a frame, in the centre of which are a number of vertical, slightly splayed spindles of wood.

Strap hinge: A hinge with a narrow, flat projection of metal secured across part of the face of the door.

Swag: A carved or painted decoration resembling a piece of fabric draped between two supports or a garland of ribbons, flowers, fruit and/or foliage. (Also known as a festoon.)

Tallboy: Tall chest of drawers, usually made in two sections.

Tallow: Animal fat.

Terracotta: Unglazed earthenware made from a mixture of clay and sand.

Thatching: Roof covering made of straw, reeds, heather or similar material.

Tongue-and-groove: A system of joining wooden boards by fitting a cut or planed projection along the side of one board into a groove in an adjacent board.

Transparent oil glaze: A viscous clear medium to which pigments are added to form a semi-transparent glaze or paint.

Trestle table: A table in which the top, made up of planks or boards, rests on trestles (two or more, made up of a horizontal beam secured on four sloping legs).

Trivet: A bracket with three projections for fixing on a grate, and used to support a pot or kettle.

Tudor: Styles of architecture and decoration during the reigns of the Tudor monarchs (1485–1601).

Vane: A revolving fan.

Victorian: Period of history spanning the reign of Queen Victoria (1837–1901). In the United States, the Victorian period, in relation to architecture and design extended up to 1910.

Wash copper: A boiler, made of copper, and used for laundry.

Wattle-and-daub: Interwoven branches or pieces of wood plastered with mud and used as a building material, usually for making walls.

Weather-boarding: Overlapping, wedge-shaped boards used as the external covering of a timber-framed structure. Known as clapboarding in the U.S.

Whitewash: Traditional paint, made of lime and water or whiting, size and water – used on walls.

Windsor chair: A traditional chair with a solid wooden seat that contains sockets into which the both the legs and the slender, spindle-shaped uprights of the back are fitted.

Woodgraining: The simulation of natural wood (particularly the grain) using paints and glazes.

Directory

KITCHEN DESIGNERS AND MANUFACTURERS

Alno (UK) Ltd
Unit 10
Hampton Farm Ind Estate
Hampton Road West
Hanworth
Middlesex TW13 6DB
Kitchens can be commissioned in a range of styles, including Art Nouveau and Art Deco. Also produce a "Pastoral Collection" of country kitchen furniture.

Arc Linea
164 Brompton Road
London SW3 1HW
Specialize in freestanding, Italian/Mediterranean style.

Arena
Bartlemas Farmhouse
Bartlemas
Oxford OX4 2AD
Kitchens designed to order, in sympathy with architectural features of the house.

Brookmans
Fairholme Works
Jawbone Hill
Oughtibridge
Sheffield S30 3HW
Custom-made kitchens based on traditional designs and made by established cabinetmakers.

Bulthaup
37 Wigmore Street
London W1H 9LD
Modernist and post-Modernist kitchens, including units to take large commercial appliances.

C P Hart
Newnham Terrace
Hercules Road
London SE1 7DR
Wooden and painted kitchens in a wide range of finishes and made to traditional and modern designs.

Christian Kitchens
4 Old Market Place
Altrincham
Cheshire WA14 4NP
English country-style kitchens, in woods such as maple, oak and pine.

Cotteswood of Oxfordshire
Station Road
Chipping Norton
Oxfordshire OX7 5HN
Traditional kitchens and furniture made from maple, oak, cherry or pine, with limed or painted finishes.

Crabtree Kitchens
The Twickenham Centre
Norcutt Road
Twickenham
Middlesex TW2 6SR
Traditional-style kitchens, notably Shaker-style.

Crown Products
(System Sterling Kitchens)
Eddington
Herne Bay
Kent CT6 5TR
Traditional and modern kitchens with a versatile selection of interior fittings.

Gary Mowlem & Co
Ouseburn Building
Albion Row
Newcastle upon Tyne
NE6 5LL
Hand-built kitchens made from woods such as maple.

Graham Woodcraft
6 Church Farm Workshops
Hatley St George
Sandy
Bedfordshire SG19 3HP
Unfitted kitchen furniture handmade from ash with polished granite worktops.

Hedley James
Roses Farm
Gallants Lane
East Farleigh
Maidstone
Kent ME15 OLG

Custom-made kitchens, including a freestanding range with cook's benches and pantry cupboards.

Henslowe and Fox
Horndon Industrial Park
West Hendon
Brentwood
Essex CM13 3HP
Fitted kitchens from traditional period designs in limed oak and various painted finishes (many typical of the 18th century).

Hygrove Kitchens
152–4 Merton Road
Wimbledon
London SW19 1EH
Custom-built kitchens with traditional finishes.

John Lewis of Hungerford
High Street
Hungerford
Berkshire RG17 OEA
Traditional custom-made kitchens, built-in or freestanding and in a wide choice of natural woods and painted finishes.

Johnny Grey & Co
Fyning Copse
Rogate
Petersfield
Hampshire GU31 5DH
Hand-built natural wood and painted kitchens (many with dedicated work areas), combining modern technology with traditional craftsmanship and design.

Just Kitchens
41 Wigmore Street
London W1H 9LE
Traditional kitchens, including Shaker-style, painted and unpainted, built-in or freestanding.

Keith Gray & Co
Great Priory Farm
Panfield
Braintree, Essex

Custom-made and individually designed traditional-style kitchens.

Luke Hughes
1 Stukely Street
London WC2 5LT
Custom-made wooden kitchen furniture.

Magnet
Allington Way
Darlington
Co. Durham DL1 4XT
Produce flat-pack as well as pre-assembled kitchens, including a Shaker-inspired design.

Mark Wilkinson
Mark Wilkinson Furniture
Overton House
High Street
Bromham
Chipppenham
Wiltshire SN15 2HA
Distinctive range of custom-made, natural wood and distressed painted kitchens, including the distinctive Santa Fé and neo-Classical Etruscan designs.

Martin Moore & Co
28 Church Street
Altrincham
Cheshire WA14 4DW
Custom-built traditional kitchens and freestanding furniture in a range of natural wood finishes.

Miele Company
Fairacres
Marcham Road
Abingdon
Oxfordshire OX14 1TW
Modern and traditional designs, plus a range of integrated appliances.

Mike Chalon
The Plaza
535 King's Road
London SW10
Antique and reproduction country-style furniture.

Newcastle Furniture Company
128 Walham Green Court
Moore Park Road
London SW6 4DG
Fitted and unfitted kitchens, in natural wood and painted finishes, including Shaker-inspired units.

Penny's Mill
Nunney Frome
Somerset BA11 4NP
Custom-made kitchens in woods like maple and ash.

Plain English
The Long House Design Company
Tannery Road
Combs
Stowmarket
Suffolk 1P14 2EL
Traditional kitchens with authentic English detailing and a wide range of paint colours and finishes.

Rhode Design
86 Stoke Newington Church Street
London N16 0AP
Produce a range of traditional style kitchens in natural woods and MDF, and up to 17 different paint colours. Includes various freestanding pieces in New England style.

Robinson and Cornish
Southway House
Oakwood Close
Roundswell
Barnstaple
Devon EX3 3NJ
Made-to-measure traditional kitchens and freestanding furniture.

Romsey Cabinetmakers
Great Bridge Business Park
Budds Lane
Romsey
Hampshire SO51 0HA
Produce a range of fitted and unfitted kitchens.

The Shaker Shop
25 Harcourt Street
London W1
Shaker-style painted wooden kitchens and furniture; also baskets, peg rails and other accessories.

Siematic Kitchen Furniture
Osprey House
Rookery Court
Primett Road
Stevenage
Hertfordshire SG1 3EE
Produce a range of modern and traditional kitchens with integrated accessories and fittings.

Simple Kitchens
94 Waterford Road
Fulham
London SW6 2HA
Hand-made kitchens with traditional mouldings, primed ready for painting.

Smallbone & Co (Devizes) Limited
Hopton Industrial Estate
London Road
Devizes
Wiltshire SN10 2EU
High-quality custom-built kitchens. Choose from natural wood or hand-painted kitchens from the fitted or unfitted ranges.

Somerset Country Furniture
The Old Chapel
Church Street
Ilchester
Somerset BA22 8LN
Specialize in designing and making country-style furniture and kitchens; many items painted and distressed to create an authentic rustic finish.

The Treske Shop
5 Barmouth Road
London SW18 2DT
Natural wood and painted kitchens, and a range of freestanding furniture.

Underwood Kitchens
Lawn Farm Business Centre
Grendon Underwood
Bucks HP18 0QX
Hand-crafted kitchens using traditional English designs, in pine, limed oak and maple. Also produce freestanding furniture.

Watts & Wright
114a Wolverhampton Road
Walsall
West Midlands WS2 8PR
Cabinet makers who make traditional kitchens in a range of natural wood and painted finishes.

Whitton Wood Design
37 Crown Road
St Margarets
Twickenham
Middlesex TW1 3EJ
Custom-built kitchens and freestanding furniture in maple, limed oak, pine, ash and cherry wood.

Wood Workshop
21 Canterbury Grove
London SE27 0NT
Builders of fitted kitchens in hardwoods and traditional styles – Victorian, Arts and Crafts and Art Deco.

Woodstock Furniture
23 Packenham Street
London WC1X 0LB
Solid wooden kitchens and furniture in styles ranging from Art Deco to Gothic.

KITCHENWARE

Andrew and Joanna Young
Common Farm
Sunstead Road
Lower Gresham
Norwich NR11 8RE
Hand-potted kitchen and domestic stoneware in brown and green glazes.

Brass and Traditional Sinks Ltd
Devauden Green
Nr Chepstow
Gwent NP6 6PL
Solid brass, chrome and nickel-plate kitchen taps in a range of period styles; plus traditional glazed earthenware, French farmhouse sinks, cast-iron and stainless steel sinks.

Copperstones Kitchenware
High Street
Marlborough
Wiltshire
Specialist suppliers of kitchen wares, available through mail order.

David Mellor
4 Sloane Square
London SW1
Cooking utensils and tablewares.

Divertimenti
45-47 Wigmore Street
London W1H 9LE and
139-141 Fulham Road
South Kensington
London SW3 6SD
A wide range of cooking utensils and tableware.

The French Kitchen Shop
42 Westbourne Grove
London W2
Pottery from England, Spain, France and Italy, and kitchen equipment.

Kitchenalia
The Old Bakery
36 Inglewhite Road
Longridge
Preston
Lancs PR3 3JS
Specialist shop for antique and new kitchenware.

ANTIQUES

Ann Lingard
Ropewalk Antiques
Ropewalk
Rye, Sussex
Antique pine furniture and kitchenalia.

Below Stairs
103 High Street
Hungerford
Berkshire
Good selection of kitchenware and some lighting.

Christina Bishop
Westway
Portobello Road
London W11
A large selection of kitchenware from 1850–1950.

The Dining Room Shop
62-64 White Hart Lane
Barnes
London SW13
*Antique furniture, china
and porcelain, table linen
and kitchenalia.*

The Dog House
309 Bloxwich Road
Walsall
West Midlands
*A large selection of antique
and reproduction furniture,
china, period lighting and
kitchenware.*

Guimon Mounter
Baskers Farm
Dulford
Devon
*Pine furniture, including
some very early pieces.*

Keith Skeel Antiques
7-9 Elliot Place
Islington
London N1
Antique kitchen furniture.

Lunn Antiques
86 New Kings Road
London SW6
*Antique table linen, lace
and other textiles*

No 7 Antiques
7 Nantwich Road
Woore
Nr Crewe
*Country furniture and
kitchenalia.*

The Pot Board
30 King Street
Carmarthen
Dyfed
Wales
*Antique pine furniture and
kitchenware.*

Robert Young Antiques
68 Battersea Bridge Road
London SW11 3AG
*Country furniture and
kitchenalia.*

Wakelin & Linfield
10 New Street
Petworth
West Sussex
Antique country furniture.

TILES, FLOORS AND WORKTOPS

Amtico
Head Office and Factory
Kingfield Road
Coventry CV6 5PL
*Exceptionally high quality
vinyl floors, simulating tra-
ditional materials – marble,
wood, brick and slate.*

Candy Tiles
Heathfield
Newton Abbot
Devon TQ12 6RF
*Manufacturers of reproduc-
tion period floor tiles.*

Castelnau Tiles
175 Church Road
Barnes
London SW13 9R
*Stockists of reproduction
period wall and floor tiles.*

Crucial Trading
77 Westbourne Park Road
London W2 4BX
*Wide range of natural floor
coverings, including sea-
grass, coir, sisal and rush.*

Decorative Tile Works
Jackfield Tile Museum
Ironbridge
Telford
Shropshire TF8 7AW
*Specialists in reproduction
19th-century English tiles.*

Dennis Ruabon Ltd
Haford Tileries
Ruabon
Wrexham
Clwyd LL14 6ET
*Manufacturers of a wide
selection of tiles – many traditional "paver" shapes,
such as "bats", "sinters"
and "quoirns", which can
be laid to create geometric
tiling patterns.*

Diana Hall
1 Thatched Cottage
Ilford
Lewes
Sussex BN7 3EW
*Medieval and Victorian
encaustic tiles for floor
restorations.*

Fired Earth
Twyford Mill
Oxford Road
Adderbury
Oxfordshire OX17 3HP
*Terracotta, slate and lime-
stone floor tiles, and tradi-
tional wall tiles.*

**The Hardwood Flooring
Company**
Canada House
Blackwood Road
West Hampstead
London NW6 1RZ
*Large stock of new and
reclaimed floors made from
hardwoods such as oak,
ash, beech, maple, teak,
mahogany and pitch-pine.*

H & R Johnson Tiles Ltd
Highgate Tile Works
Tunstall
Stoke on Trent
Staffordshire T6 4JX
*Wide range of period-style
tiles, including encaustic.*

Interior Ceramics
3 York Street
Twickenham
Middlesex TQ1 3JZ
*Comprehensive selection of
ceramic tiles, marble, terracotta and slate; Victorian
reproduction and hand-
painted tiles a speciality.*

John Burgess Tiles
Unit B25
Maws Craft Centre
Jackfield
Shropshire TF8 7LS
*Reproduction Victorian and
Art Nouveau tiles.*

Kenneth Clark Ceramics
The North Wing
Southover Grange
Southover Road
Lewes
East Sussex BN17 1TP
*Manufacturers and stockists
of an extensive range of
reproduction tiles; also
stock some original tiles.*

Marston and Langinger
192 Ebury Street
London SW1N 8UP
Selection of period tiles.

The Original Tile Co
23a Howe Street
Edinburgh EH3 6TF
*Wide range of tiles – marble,
terracotta, natural stone,
and hand-painted, in many
period styles.*

Paris Ceramics
543 Battersea Park Road
London SW11
*Specialize in restoring/laying
antique terracotta and stone
floors from France, Spain,
England and Holland.*

Scandafloor
Lytham St Annes
Lancashire
*Traditional plank, strip and
parquet floors.*

UK Marble Ltd
21 Burcott Road
Hereford HR4 9LW
*Marble and granite for
floors and worktops.*

Victorian Woodworks
139 Church Walk
London N16
*Specializes in laying all
types of wooden floors, also
undertakes restoration work.*

**York Handmade Brick
Company**
Forest Lane
Alne
North Yorkshire YO6 2LU
*Manufacturers of handmade
bricks and terracotta tiles.*

STOVES AND RANGES

**Aga-Rayburn
Glynwed Consumer &
Building Products Ltd**
PO Box 30
Ketley
Telford TF1 4DD
*Distributors of an extensive
range of Aga and Rayburn
cast-iron ranges.*

Calfire (Chirk) Ltd
Unit One
Acorn Industrial Estate
Holyhead Road
Chirk, Clwyd LL14 5NA
*Gas, oil and multi-fuel
combination cookers.*

Coalbrookdale
Glynwed Products Ltd
PO Box 30
Ketley
Telford
Shropshire TF1 4DD
*Suppliers of multi-fuel
cast-iron stoves.*

Country Cookers
5 Sherford Street
Bromyard
Herefordshire HR7 4DL
*Huge selection of new and
reconditioned cookers and
ranges.*

Imperial UK
Fairacres
Marcham Road
Abingdon
Oxfordshire OX14 1TW
*Manufacture a wide range
of appliances.*

Lacanche
Fourneaux de France Ltd
62 Westbourne Grove
London W2 5SH
*High-quality kitchen
ranges; professional and
domestic quality.*

**TRADITIONAL PAINT
SUPPLIERS/SPECIALIST
DECORATORS**

Cole & Son Ltd
18 Mortimer Street
London W1A 4BU
*Stock period paints,
including Georgian gray
and Queen Anne white.*

Craig and Rose
172 Leith Walk
Edinburgh EH6 5EP
*Manufacturers and suppli-
ers of traditional varnishes,
including extra pale
dead-flat varnish.*

Cy-Près
14 Bells Close
Brigstock
Kettering
Northants
*Makers of traditional soft
distemper in a range of
24 colours, manufactured
using natural earth
pigments.*

Design Archives
79 Walton Stree
London SW3 5EL
*Offer a wide range of tradi-
tional paint finishes.*

E Ploton (Sundries) Ltd
273 Archway Road
London N6 5AA
*Suppliers of a wide range of
paints, varnishes and decorating equipment.*

Green and Stone
259 Kings Road
London SW3 5EL
*Stock decorating materials,
stencils and glazes.*

Heart of the Country
Home Farm
Swinfen
Near Lichfield
Staffordshire
*A wide range of American
period-style paints, includ-
ing "Williamsburg" butter-
milk paint colours.*

Henryk Terpilowski
22a Station Road
London NW10
*Decorator specializing in
marbling, woodgraining
and a wide range of traditional finishes.*

John T Keep & Sons Ltd
15 Theobold's Road
London WC1X 8FN
*Suppliers of transparent oil
glaze, universal stains and
artist's pigments.*

J W Bollom Group
PO Box 76
Croydon Road
Beckenham
Kent BR3 4BL
*Manufacturers and suppli-
ers of a wide range of
paints, varnishes, stains,
and waxes.*

Mark Done
3 Mount Fort Terrace
Barnsbury Square
London N1 1JJ
*Decorator specializing in
a wide range of finishes,
including wood graining,
marbling and antiquing.*

National Trust
c/o Farrow and Ball
Vodens Trading Estate
Wimborne
Dorset
*Seven types of traditional
paints, in 57 different
colourways.*

Papers and Paints
4 Park Walk
London SW10
*Produce 112 colours in their
"Historic Range", and dis-
tempers in 28 colours.*

Pavilion Originals Ltd
6A Howe Street
Edinburgh EH3 6TD
*Manufacturers of fine
specialist paints, glazes
and stencilling materials
(including classic and
contemporary stencils).*

Potmolen Paints
27 Woodstock Industrial
Estate
Warminster BA12 9DX
*Supply conservation grade
limewashes, casein and
oil-bound distemper, and
bio-degradable paint
stripper.*

Rose of Jericho
Dene Corby
Northhants NN17 3EJ
*Traditional paints, renders
and plasters, including
limewash.*

Tom Hickman
10 Bath Street
Frome
Somerset
*Murals and stencils,to
commission.*

PERIOD LIGHTING

Chelsom Ltd
Heritage House
Clifton Road
Blackpool
Lancashire FY4 4QA
*Suppliers of a wide range of
reproduction lighting,
including Georgian,
Regency, period American,
Art Deco, Art Nouveau and
Victorian designs.*

**Christopher Wray
Lighting**
600 Kings Road
London SW6 2DX
*Stock a vast selection of
reproduction period lighting
equipment and accessories.*

**End of the Day Lighting
Company**
44 Parkway
London NW1
*Stockists of traditional
lighting, including ceiling
pendants and wall brackets.*

**Fritz Fryer Decorative
Antique Lighting**
12 Brookend Street
Ross on Wye
Herefordshire HR9 7EG
*Specialize in decorative
antique lighting, especially
1850–1920.*

Jones
194 Westbourne Grove
London W11
*Restored antique lighting
from 1860–1960.*

**Kensington Lighting
Company**
34 and 59 Kensington
Church Street
London W8 4HA
Traditional lighting.

Stiffkey Lamp Shop
Nells Road
Stiffkey
Townsend
Norfolk NR23 1AJ
*Specialize in the conversion
of original gas lamps to
electricity, and stock a wide
range of antique and
reproduction lamps.*

Sugg Lighting Ltd
65 Gatwick Road
Crawley
West Sussex RH10 2YU
*Manufacturers of gas and
electric lighting in a wide
range of traditional styles.
They also offer a refurbish-
ment service.*

Index

ACKNOWLEDGEMENTS

The author and publishers would like to thank the following organisations and individuals for providing the photographs used in this book:

Arcaid/Richard Bryant
Arena
Belling Appliances Limited
Brass and Traditional Sinks
Brookmans Design Group
Bruce Boehner: Kitchen, La Casa Nueva, Workman and
Temple Family Homestead Museum
Copperstones
Country Life
Crabtree Kitchens
Czech and Speake
Daily Mail/Solo
Fired Earth
Fourneaux de France/Lacanche Stoves
Keith Gray and Co. Limited
C. P. Hart
Hedley James
International Interiors/Paul Ryan
Imperial Appliances
Just Kitchens Western Limited
John Lewis of Hungerford
Martin Moore Handmade Kitchens
Mekon Products Limited
Miele
MJM Publishing projects/Caroline Brown, Geoff Dann, John Helfrick,
Martin Miller
National Trust Photographic Library/Andreas von Einsiedel
Newcastle Furniture Limited
Reed International Books Ltd/Michael Crockett, Ian B. Jones, James Merrell,
Martin Norris, Kim Sayer
Smallbone of Devizes Handcrafted Kitchens
Stonell
Mark Wilkinson Furniture Limited
Woodstock Furniture Limited

Thanks also to Pavilion Originals Limited for providing the
Charles Rennie Mackintosh-inspired stencil and stencil paints.